AF570199

HOW TO PAINT IN WATER-COLOURS

HOW TO PAINT IN WATER-COLOURS

by

PAUL WYETH, A.R.C.A., R.B.A.

with a Foreword by
FREDERICK BEDDINGTON

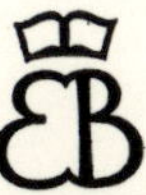

ELEK BOOKS
GREAT JAMES STREET, LONDON

Copyright © Paul Wyeth 1958
Published 1958 *by*
ELEK BOOKS LIMITED
14 *Great James Street*
*London W.*1

and simultaneously in Canada by
The Ryerson Press
299 *Queen Street West*
Toronto 2B
Canada

Printed in Great Britain by
Page Bros. (Norwich) Ltd.
Norwich

CONTENTS

FOREWORD

No doubt it is the intention of the reader to seek help from Mr. Wyeth in his pursuit of the Art of Water-colour. Since the author has clearly understood his task, no introduction is necessary to a work easily understood and economically expressed, and it is merely a pleasant duty to introduce the author.

One is often asked the question about the pursuit of art—how much depends on gift and how much can be learned by hard work in producing results? When I first knew Paul Wyeth he appeared to me to be the most naturally gifted artist I had ever met. Not only did he appear to be unconscious of this fact; difficulties seemed not to exist for him. Today I see how consciously he has worked to produce this apparent ease of expression and I am impressed throughout his book by his extraordinarily practical understanding of the beginner's difficulties. It would be hard to think of any normally gifted artist who could not learn something of practical use from this work and for all those who derive pleasure from painting it will prove a mine of information, a sound guide and a stimulus and, I hope, often a desire to contradict.

When the lessons given here have been mastered, we must remember that a time may come when they may all be neglected and thrown away and that then the reader may start all over again breaking all rules here laid down. He may then produce a work of art—but he must have, need I add, just a touch of genius.

FRED BEDDINGTON.

April 1958.
Wildenstein & Co., Ltd.

INTRODUCTION

ALMOST everyone, it seems, today has a brush in his or her hands, and is happily engaged in the pursuit of pleasure and the beautiful. Flower painting, landscape, portrait, composition—nothing is too hard or too difficult for them. Exhibitors throughout the country tell the story better than any words of mine; for the great majority of exhibitors are "Sunday painters". Now, of course, they are Monday, Tuesday and every-day-of-the-week painters. Once the magic of painting has touched you, it seems there is no escape. For some it has become an interesting hobby; for many others the greatest pleasure and for some a new life.

Everyone wants to paint, yet those who are prepared to learn the art the traditional way, which admittedly is not the easiest, are certainly in the minority. By traditional I mean the way practised by every master of water-colour of any distinction during the past three hundred years. De Wint, Gainsborough, Claude, Cotman, Turner—what magic in these names! For them as for you, there is no easy way, which surely makes the prize all the more glittering in the end. But of all these thousands upon thousands of Sunday painters only a small percentage have realized the joy and thrill of "pure water-colour painting". Most of the others will have run ahead—at the beginning—in the *wrong direction.* For so many aspirants believe they can skip the trouble to learn something of drawing first, and dive straight into painting. That is why so many people become disheartened after a while and give it up. That is, alas, why it is essential to acquire some technical foundation to your painting in the form of drawing.

MATERIALS: COLOURS, BRUSHES, PAPER

ONE of the reasons why so many people are becoming attracted to painting with water-colours is that the materials are inexpensive and light. An overcoat pocket will hold everything—paint-box and water-colour block as well. At the same time, the materials need a minimum of preparation or effort to clear away after a session of painting. There are no easels to put up, no palettes to lay out, and no large and cumbersome equipment. All this makes it a most light and compact medium to practise out of doors. How often on a walking tour, or cycling, you suddenly come across a view of wood and river, mountain and sky. . . . How convenient to have everything you need ready for use in a matter of minutes. Again, unlike oils, there is none of the worry about waiting for the colours to dry.

The choice of paper is of prime importance. Consider the quality of its surface—neither smooth nor rough—and its weight—heavy or light. Although, in the end, personal preference or taste will make you decide on one paper rather than on another, your choice should always be made with a particular end in view. For instance, should you decide to make a lot of small slight sketches—quickly, out of doors, perhaps in a market place, or by the river—you will not require a very heavy paper but perhaps a sketch block (for water-colour) of 14 in. by 10 in. On the other hand, should you set yourself down on Richmond Hill to make a panorama of the sweeping view over the Thames, you will require a much stouter and heavier material. Again, the lighter the paper, the greater tendency it will have to "buckle" when you apply washes, whereas a really heavy paper such as 300-lb. Whatman will not buckle at all with normal use when painting out of doors. Generally speaking, a Nott surface paper will be found best for most purposes.

Remember that very smooth or lightweight paper will begin to buckle as soon as you lay your first wash on it. This increases your difficulties tenfold, making further work very difficult, and often unpleasant.

If you work on the paper mentioned above you will find that it has many advantages, not least amongst them being that it will need no mounting; secondly, you will be able to scrub out any part or detail of your painting without making a hole in the paper or damaging its surface for further work. The details of how and when to wash or sponge up will be dealt with in the next chapter.

You cannot always judge with any degree of accuracy just how a particular painting will go. It may start quite well and everything may be going on fine enough. Then a bit of cloud or sea or foreground may give trouble. For instance, you may not be satisfied with your first rendering of a stretch of water or the reflections in a mill pond, or possibly you go wrong when putting in a telegraph pole or some such detail. You will then want to try it again. In such cases the professional water-colourist may well start all over again rather than cause a mess, which more often than not leads to muddy colouring. But for the beginner-amateur, this is not necessary or to be recommended. You are out to learn as much as you possibly can and you will do so every bit as much by your failures as by your successes. The thing is, to know what to do when a mistake has been made. On thin paper, you will have to let it go because to play about on thin paper is just not possible without going through the surface.

So much for paper. Generally, anything between 200–300 lb. Nott surface.

Next, your paint-box! This is something you must choose yourself. Remember that you will want to carry it about. It must therefore be compact but possess as large a palette as possible with plenty of room for your colours. Of these you need the following:

Cadmium Yellow
Yellow Ochre
Vermilion
Light Red or Venetian Red
Alizarin-Crimson
Raw Umber
Black
Cobalt
Prussian Blue

With these nine colours there is practically no limit to what can be done once you are familiar with them, both individually and collectively. And this is what you will first be required to do—make yourself familiar with your colours.

Next, your brushes must be of such a variety, in size and quality, that, with a little experience, you will know which one to use for any specific detail. You will need to begin with one large sable—Whistler Super Ox. No. 14—for washes, skies, clouds, distances, foregrounds and other large areas of colour. You will also need No. 8 to No. 10, if possible, and two smaller brushes, about No. 5 and possibly a No. 2.

A piece of sponge and a water-bottle are also essential. A metal flask, if obtainable, is the ideal type, because as it is something that will be carried about a good deal, a glass one may get damaged or even broken. This can be something of a catastrophe when, on arrival at your destination, you find there is no other source of getting water. A hip flask in aluminium is the ideal water container.

Water is something that you will come to appreciate if, for example, you suddenly find yourself without any more—just when you are in the middle of a passage of sky-painting, or any other painting for that matter. I have always found a thermos flask very useful on a picnic for carrying a reserve supply of water.

A knapsack is a very useful part of your equipment if you intend to do much painting out of doors. A stool of the three-legged variety is also to be recommended, as it fits comfortably into a knapsack.

Your paper, if in the form of a water-colour block, will be usable just as it is, without your having to carry a small drawing board as well. But if your paper is loose, then you should try to get a stout piece of cardboard or hardboard on which to clip it. Again, you will find working out of doors much simpler if you get into the habit of always working on a set size, say 14 in. by 10 in., which is quite ample for most purposes.

Thus you will come to appreciate working in a given dimension. Should you wish to paint something smaller, turning the board upright will give two sheets of approximately the same proportions, but half the size.

An easel is not necessary, and I would suggest that from the start you familiarize yourself with finding a suitable base for your board and paper, either by resting it on your knee or on a piece of wall or branch of a tree, or anything else that may be handy. One last point: you will need a pencil to block or sketch in the main lines and forms of whatever you are about to paint. Also a piece of eraser or rubber, although I would not recommend the use of it too often. It is always much better to try to draw correctly from the start without having to depend on corrections to get it right.

HOW TO BEGIN

I MENTIONED the necessity in the previous chapter for some knowledge of drawing; I would now like to be more explicit. This book has been arranged with the beginner in mind, but with the beginner in water-colour particularly, and not for the person with no previous experience whatsoever in drawing. There have been people with no previous knowledge of drawing, who have made immediate progress when they took up painting. But they have been very few indeed, and the average beginner would do well to familiarize himself with drawing first and water-colour painting second. This does not mean that he should be an accomplished draughtsman, but he must at least be able to draw those forms which he intends painting with a reasonable degree of accuracy, and do this with a fair knowledge of proportion and perspective.

It is true that painting is drawing with a brush, and in my book *How to Paint in Oils* I mentioned that some schools of painting have taught their pupils to start drawing with the brush rather than with a pencil. But this applied to oil painting, where you can go on painting over, making as many corrections as necessary without spoiling the finished effect. With water-colours it is very different, because you have to preserve that fresh, spontaneous quality, with its transparency and limpidity, and this is lost when you make corrections one over the other.

Too much pencil work is to be discouraged, but one cannot lay down any hard and fast rules, as one student may have a totally different "eye" on the subject than another and wish to utilize his "scaffolding" more than the next. He may have seen the water-colours of Jongkind or Boudin or Girtin and desire to tackle something on the same lines. This is indeed a healthy sign providing he uses his intelligence as much as his eyes. To copy slavishly the work of a master is no use and will tell you nothing. You must attempt to use his mind and eye and probe the method of work—from sky, shadows, stonework, trees, water, etc. This is the intelligent approach. Side by side with the study of the master-work must go practice in tackling nature at first-hand—using the simplest forms such as kitchen pots and pans, apples, peas, jugs, books. Then, by the study of nature in all her moods, lighting, colour and coincidences, can the student be said to be laying a sound foundation upon which to paint in water-colours.

Now acquaint yourself thoroughly with the colours in the box. With all nine colours the range is almost infinite, and you would possibly do well to use only three or four for the first few attempts. Providing you have had some little practice in drawing, you should soon be able to produce a reasonable effort in water-colour.

First take a large piece of stout paper—cartridge will do for this purpose—and clip or pin it to your drawing board. Damp the paper by wetting the sponge and then gently squeezing most of the water out. Rub it all over the surface of the paper. There are three reasons for this: it will eliminate a lot of buckling and enable the colour to flow better from your brush, and at the same time give the edge of each brush mark a certain softness. The wetter the paper, the softer your colour edge will be. Then squeeze out on to your palette (unless your paint-box is of the "pan" variety) a little ivory black. Using your longest brush, dip the brush first into the water and next into the colour: mix a little on your palette (or in one of the single trays) until you are satisfied it is well mixed. Then "play"; for I cannot think the use of any other word would fit quite so well. "Play" about on your paper, making sketches large and small. See how you can "manage" a full brush of colour without dropping it anywhere but where you want it.

When you have experimented in this fashion for ten minutes you might consider making a "wash". For this you will require an area on your paper of about 6 in. by 6 in. to start with. This is a very simple exercise in the use and manipulation of the brush when "loaded" with colour. Your board or block should of course be at an angle of about 30° to 45° so that the mixture on the brush flows properly and does not run into puddles! With plenty of the mixture (black and water) in your pan, take a full brush of it and make a stroke across the topmost edge of the area you are going to cover. Taking another full brush as before, repeat directly below, but touching the first stroke, from left to right. Then repeat until you are down to the bottom of the paper. If you find that it runs or trickles ahead of you down the paper, don't worry about it at first, but learn from it how to become proficient at laying a clean wash without letting it get out of control. Providing you are quick in covering over the "run" or trickle, it will not show darker afterwards but melt into the general colour. You will need to experiment rather a lot during the first days!

Next practise diluting the strong black colour in your pan with a little water, in various quantities, so that you get as many greys or gradations between black and the white of your paper as you possibly can. There are many more of these than you will need to know but at this stage you will want at least four, or rather experience in being able to mix the four whenever you require them.

Now I want you to do the same exercise, if not with all

the remaining eight colours, then at least with the primary colours:

Cadmium Yellow
Vermilion
Prussian Blue

As you move from one to the other you will find each colour separate to do.

You should now begin to feel at home with your brush, paper and paints, sufficiently, at least, to allow you to progress to *Colour Mixing*.

Colour mixing is not quite so difficult as the beginner probably thinks. No two people will see colour in quite the same way. To some yellow is slightly green: to others, orange; and a slight difference between light and dark takes place with most colours, from one person's vision to another. Colour mixing is an art that can only be mastered if the pupil is really interested.

Apart from the colours I have recommended, you will produce an unlimited number of other colours by the careful mixing together of these nine. If you begin by gaining practice in mixing your red and yellow together in equal amounts, you will get an excellent orange. Red and blue—again in equal parts—will produce a very good purple. Blue and yellow, in equal parts, will give green; blue, yellow and vermilion all together in equal parts, a good brown.

Now practise mixing some of the other nine together. Mix your crimson with Prussian for a deep purple. Mix yellow ochre with Prussian for a deep cabbage-like green.

Try using a dry and then a very wet colour simply by adding a little more water to your colour for the latter.

Now draw in pencil a dozen or more irregular shapes varying from a square to a triangle, from a trapezian to a full circle, petal shapes and star shapes, etc. Paint into these as accurately as you are able to. A smaller brush will be easier, but I recommend you to use as large a brush as you can possibly manage. This will make you exercise care and accuracy which will be of great help when it comes to tackling detail later on.

The beginner should now choose any colour reproduction he can find, preferably one in bright strong colours and, of course, with a minimum of detail.

Attempt to copy this. First use a slight pencil line to draw it in. This will make it simpler to lay the various colours in their correct place. Later you might try doing the same painting without the use of guide lines. The control of your colour and washes will have to be great indeed.

Perhaps I should mention here that there is no need to hasten the drying of each colour as they lay next to each other. If you are careful you will lay each area of colour next to its neighbour without actually touching it; that is, a tiny strip of your white paper will separate them. This was a method used to great advantage by John Sell Cotman. (See page 52.)

It has certain advantages over the more usual ones in that you need not wait for any particular part to dry before applying your next touch of colour. On the other hand, if you do wish to hasten the drying of any particular piece of colour, you can always use a piece of clean blotting paper. Naturally you will find that in so doing the colour will become probably much lighter than intended. This you must allow for. Experience will teach you the proper strength.

The next step is to find yourself the largest and best colour reproductions of the masters you possibly can—Turner, Cotman, Constable, Wilson Steer. Pin these up beside you and practise copying passages from them to the limit of your patience and ability. Do not set out to copy the picture as a whole but rather try to gain an intimate idea of how certain masters have gone about certain problems.

Find a patch of cloud or sky in one; in another, look for hills, water, barns; in another, stonework or ships in port. In fact, look at everything or anything that touches your interest and set yourself to find out how it was done. Acquaint yourself with water-colour paintings by Boudin, Jongkind, and Cézanne. See how each in his different way solved the problem of colour, tone and light. Yet all of them have in common the quality, freshness, transparency and limpidity of pure water-colour painting. All these treasures are yours to have and to study, to criticize and to improve on, if possible.

The best effects in water-colour are only achieved by a direct "do-it-in-one-go" approach. No amount of tickling or niggling with a brush will ever equal in freshness a patch of colour applied freely and left wet and clean.

Of course, you can drop other colours into wet colour to change the colour slightly or for some special reason, such as sky or cloud, sea and distant hills, into which you want to try a dash of warmer colour, or cooler colour, as the case may be.

In fact, it is a good idea to practise dropping colour into a previously applied colour before the former has fully dried. This is one of the technical tricks of the trade.

The great beauty of water-colour is its transparency and this is lost as soon as one attempts to work over a colour that has dried out. So if you wish to make a blue warmer, or red more bright, or green a little stronger or lighter, do so while the colour is wet, if possible.

But speed is essential. This is where the practice gained earlier in laying on simple washes and filling the irregular shapes with accuracy, will come in handy.

CHOOSING A SUBJECT

WE are now familiar with our material and able to tackle something a little more ambitious perhaps than pots and pans. This brings me to the question of composition and, of course, subject-matter.

When the student-painter is occupied with the problems of colour, he is inclined to see colour everywhere, to the detriment of tone; when dealing with tone, he sees tone everywhere, to the detriment of colour and drawing. When thinking of composition he will begin to see composition in everything. In this instance he will be right to do so, for composition does concern everything the painter tackles. And just as the study of the masters will help with colour and tone, I would ask the student to study their compositions also. Notice how the proportion of sky to land has been carefully worked out in the work of such painters as Steer, Turner and Boudin.

You will not find nature ready with compositions that are designed for the shape of your paper. Nature is too vast and generous. It is the artist's first task to select a part from the whole, as he certainly cannot pretend to be able to paint nature in her entirety.

This is where a viewfinder, made by cutting a rectangular shape out of a piece of board or paper is of great value. Through this you can quickly see what particular part of the landscape you wish to tackle.

Adjusting the view by moving the card from left to right until you feel you have the most satisfactory composition.

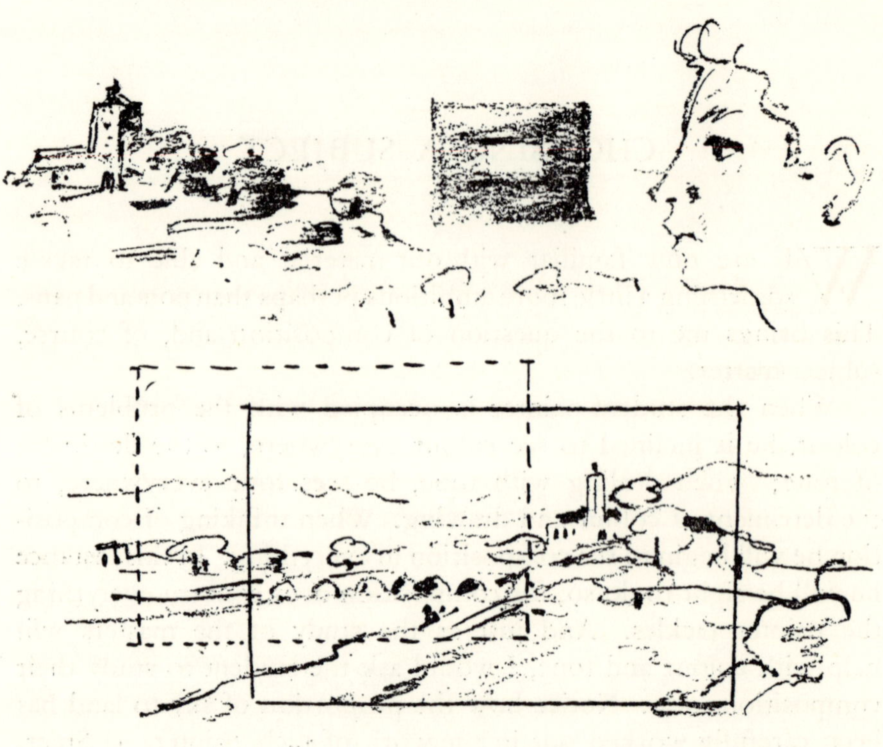

It may happen that you are faced with a large and generous piece of landscape, a panorama in fact, out of which you want to choose simply a part as shown in my diagram. There is really no limit to the number of views that can be obtained by careful selection from the whole view. Later on, you may tackle the whole lot but there are many reasons why you should start first by tackling small, less grand scenes. The experienced painter can select his view without such an aid as the plotter, and you yourself will be able with more practice to dispense with its use, just as you will drop the use of all mechanical aids as plumb lines, blue glass and diminishing glass. These aids only remind us of what our intelligence and eyes should find for themselves.

Subject-matter is a fascinating problem, especially in relation to its change with the times in which we live. You have only to see pictures of fifty and sixty years ago to see how the question of subject has been influenced by the times in which the painters lived. Certainly, the most sure and unchanging subject of all is still life. From the Italian primitives to the present day, the still life has remained as fresh and true a form of study and inspiration as anything else I can think of. Times may change but painters will always come back to still life, just as they have done in the past.

Flowers in an old jug, or seen through a glass vase, their stems greenish tendrils through the water, apples and pears, perhaps one cut open, the knife beside it, or peaches on a few leaves, perhaps on a bit of Delft ware, a napkin and a pound of cherries, red rubies on white, with a half-melon like an open mouth, its black pips making a wonderful sparkle—these things have always been a source of study and strength to artists.

And how exciting it is to arrange a still-life group!

The placing of the simplest objects can be of the greatest importance. Placed one way they can look very attractive, and placed another way—quite absurd! But always they are lovely and a joy to arrange, providing you use your intelligence; quite obviously there are some things that certainly don't go together. For instance, a lemon and an old boot look absurd together, but apples on a plate do not.

In choosing an old Staffordshire or Chelsea jug or a flute, a mandolin, or a leather-bound book, you are associating yourself with things that are in themselves lovely. Their contours, colour and texture, forms and proportions are as beautiful and functional as man could make them. In the work of the masters, you will often find an old jug or pewter tankard used time and time again, each time in a slightly different position or light than the last. Look at the still life of Velasquez, Chardin and Manet, Cézanne and William Nicholson, and you will pick up familiar objects time and time again.

As regards subject-matter, you may experiment a little to find out what is the particular field that you wish to devote your time to. It may mean, perhaps, church interiors, or railway stations, market scenes, or children at play. And though there is no sound reason why you should not go back to Greek mythology or the Bible for your subject-matter, it would probably be best, at least to begin with, to be a little less ambitious and to concentrate on the simple things you find around you in everyday life.

You may have a wish to emulate some of the past masters or at least try to. If you make a serious study of De Wint, David E. Cox, Cotman and Constable, you will find, after a short time, that the world around you will assume a similarity of colour, contour and beauty, simply because these painters have stated a great truth which can be discovered by all of us when we turn to nature. The masters will help you to see nature. Try it for a while. Look long and seriously at Constable's paintings and I am sure you will discover more about nature than you would ever do without his work, which acts as a window upon the world.

The same is true of Turner, Wilson Steer and others. Their great perception and power of observation assist us in our own humble search for the secrets of nature. In time, with more experience, you will see things around you through your own eyes and you will express them in your own way. That is precisely the purpose of this book, but before you can express yourself you can use the expressions of others to find yourself and your own way of seeing things in the world about you.

Subjects are in abundance everywhere we turn, but it is best for the student to confine himself to the simple things rather than to the difficult ones, certainly at first. As in my sketch of a beach-scene:

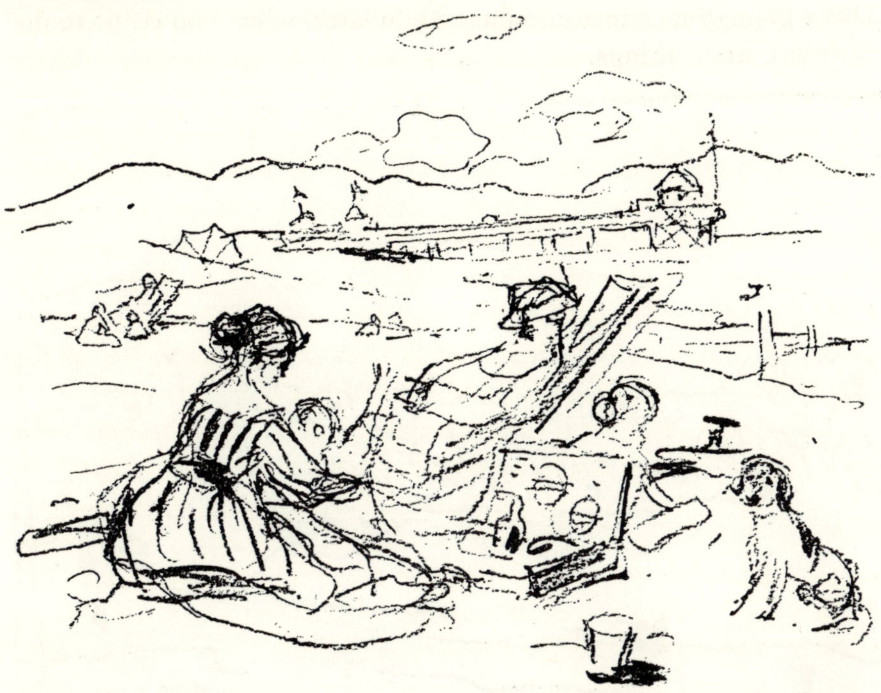

There is nothing very difficult in this, simply a stretch of beach with a little sea and distant hills, with a simple sky relieved by a little white cloud.

Or take the following sketch in which you could lightly pencil in the main shapes which are certainly simple enough, laying the various washes of colour into them, taking care that you mix your colours as near to those you find in nature. In the sketch I have indicated the numbers of colour-washes required to lay this type of scene in your picture space. There are roughly seven, and even if there were twice as many, you can see from that how few large areas of colour there are. All the detail—shadow, changes of colour and texture—can be added to these seven areas. Also, if when painting the scene before you, you start from the top and work down, as in my drawing, you will develop a certain discipline. This will be of inestimable value to you later, when you come to do more ambitious things.

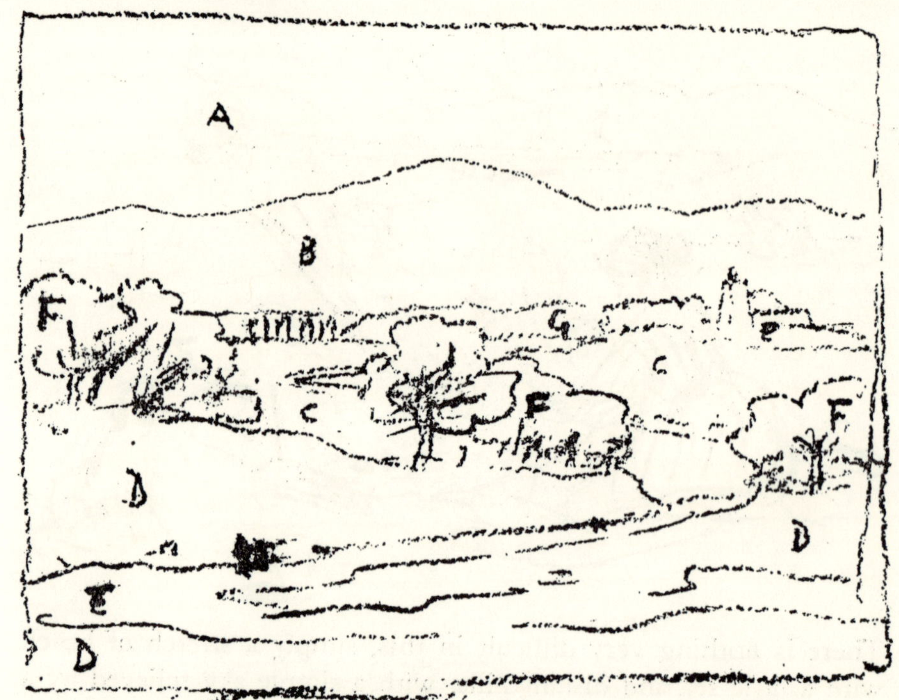

NUMBER OF MAIN WASHES—APPROXIMATELY SEVEN
A—Pale greyish blue. B—The same as A, with a little red added. C—Light green. D—Richer green than C. E—Pale Raw Sienna with a little red. F—Deep green. G—Bluish green.

These last two examples are for those interested in landscape painting. But, of course, landscape is only one form of activity. There are a hundred subjects allied to it, such as animal painting in landscape settings; farmyard scenes; cows, pigs, cattle. There is a very great choice.

This subject is not very hard to find, even for those living in London. A Green Line bus can take the Londoner into the country in half an hour. But it is much easier for those living in the country, having opportunity close at hand, to return again and again to the scene.

Here again is another subject:

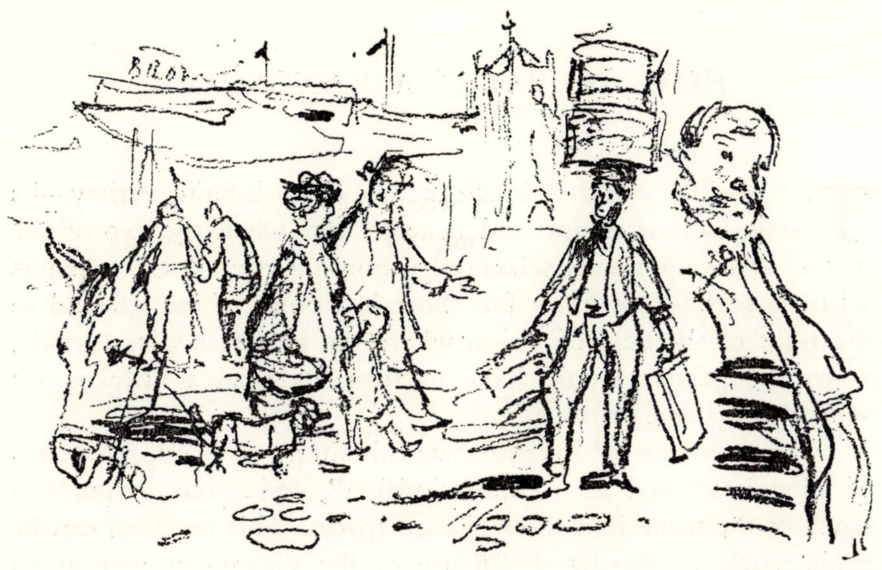

always full of interest, life and colour—the Market Scene. For this type of work the best plan is to sketch the scene with care, giving particular attention to the characters, young men in bright shirts, old women in bonnets, children, ponies, etc. etc. Note the character of the figures bending or standing or walking about, and the colours of the stalls, fruit, vegetables, boxes and costumes. Look out for any little bit of colour or gaiety—a red scarf, a box of oranges, a blue shirt, a yellow hat—or perhaps a flag or two waving, or the man with the balloons. This is perhaps one of the happiest subjects the beginner could tackle.

HOW TO PAINT A LANDSCAPE

THE visible world is inexhaustible in its infinite variety—its range, colour, shape and beauty. But when the eye of the painter seizes upon it, it seizes only upon one part of it. He paints what he sees before him. But there is a point to the left and to the right of the field of vision where the picture begins to fade, when the painter would have to turn his head a little to see squarely the scene before him.

Many students fail to appreciate this simple fact and, regardless of what is termed the "cone of vision", endeavour to put too much of the scene into their picture space. This problem can be made much simpler by skilful use of the viewfinder mentioned earlier.

What is the first thing you should do when you come to a turn of the road and see before you an avenue of trees, their branches reaching out over the road—as if to clasp the farther side—and you want to paint it? Consider it. That is, make doubly sure by using your viewfinder that the scene really is what you first thought it to be. Ask yourself: has it the makings of a design? Does it lend itself to water-colour work without any great alterations or additions? So often you will read that if you want to you can always change a detail in a landscape. This I consider bad advice from the start. The true artist should let himself be absorbed by the scene insofar as he accepts most of what nature has placed before him. Sometimes, perhaps, there are good reasons for not painting in something and at other times for slightly changing the position of something else. But one should not abuse this privilege, and should avoid doing so as much as possible.

Landscape painting as a subject occupies more than half of all the painting being done at the present time. This is borne out in many of the exhibitions up and down the country. Landscapes in sunshine and shower, fog and snow, landscapes all the year round are a great source of inspiration to the painter. Some artists wait for the spring landscape—the promise of pink and white blossom, light ethereal greens and tenderness everywhere. Others wait for the autumn, with its russet and gold colouring, or the bleakness of a winter scene with tall bare elms skirting a ploughed field. Others again wait for the coming of the snow on fence-top and guttering, window-box and country lane. Some are happy the full year long. All they ask for is a little good light and shelter from the raindrops. When the cold is such that no one will venture out, you will sometimes see an old artist huddled in a shop doorway out of the cold wind, with his little sketch-book! When the heat strikes hot and hard so that everyone wants to sleep in the shade, again there's your artist out under a straw hat with his tackle, water-colours, sketch-book and all. He is oblivious to the amazed stares of the onlookers who wonder perhaps where he finds the energy to work in the sun. But that's the point you must get quite clear to begin with—it's not work, it's pleasure! Pleasure from beginning to end.

Now let us start a landscape. Collect your water-colour gear, your hat and mac should it rain—remember this is England, not the Sudan—and follow me. Make a mental list of all your requirements and check up on them—paper, paints, brushes, water—the more the better—sponge, and let's be off.

For this trip I think perhaps we'll find what we're looking for on Hampstead Heath. Blue hills, distance, sky—a few buildings, perhaps to the right—and even a little stretch of lake.

For the purposes of demonstration I have chosen a classic landscape composition, the sort that has been repeated ten thousand times since Hobbema and Claude, yet the subject is never exhausted.

To the left a large group of trees, a smaller group to the right and also in the middle distance. The far distance itself connects the two groups of trees, with a horizontal band of blue.

The dusty earth-coloured lane leading into the foreground from the lower right winds itself out into the distance, taking the spectator with it. The problem of what to rest our tackle on is simplified here; we can squat on the grass and quite comfortably rest it on our knees.

Now what do we do first? Imagine that you are looking over my shoulder and so see how I go about it. Having damped the paper with a moist sponge I put it to one side, and in a sketch-book I sketch out the scene's main points, quite simply, as in my sketch, to become familiar with the general character of the form and shapes I am going to tackle. Perhaps by skilful use of my view-finder I find I can extend the view a little to the right. Or perhaps I can allow rather more foreground . . . as the case may be.

Having sketched a little of the scene in my sketch-book, I am much better equipped to start the painting itself. First a line, very light, using a 2-B pencil for the skyline which is placed about half-way down my paper. Next the large group of elms on the left. Thirdly, I fix the trees in the middle distance to the right; then perhaps an adjustment of the skyline, if necessary. Then back to drawing, not too heavily, but with vigour, the main features of distance—a little bit of church spire, or factory roof, housetops, etc. On to the drawing of the trees on my left. Boldly I draw in the positions of trunks and main shapes of foliage, being extra careful to place the trunks on the ground in correct relation to each other.

Observe that I am not being the least bit tender-footed about drawing in these shapes, using the pencil perhaps quite heavily here and there, wherever I feel the necessity or where my enthusiasm gets the better of me. This naturally brings about some strengthening of the lines, which is to be expected if you draw with vigour and speed.

This perhaps is the right moment to mention that your first drawing or framework, whether in ink, pencil or chalk, should be something fine in itself, with all the qualities associated with drawing and calligraphy. No one can lay down just how far you should take this preliminary framework. Practice and experience will give you the clue when to stop. All one can point out is that you are painting a water-colour, not tinting a drawing. That is, the washing of colour and the application of paint should be of greater importance than the framework in pencil that holds it, but this is something the beginner must work out for himself.

The next thing to do is to suggest with a line here and there positions of clouds, paths, or any other little feature that catches the eye. The first thing I usually do is to fix in my mind, before actually applying colour, the composition of the colour. The scaffolding gives me the linear composition, but the colour has a composition entirely of its own, for whereas a large mass of form shown with a line may well occupy more than half of our picture space, a quite small patch of violent colour may be of far greater significance. So I first make myself familiar with the colour layout or composition; using a coloured viewfinder is a mistake for beginners, as they will not readily transfer the colour seen through the viewfinder on to the white paper on which they are working.

Many books teach it is best to start with the sky and work down. Although this has certain advantages, I must say it also has a few disadvantages. For instance, perhaps the sky will not be quite right to begin with, that is, the composition of cloud and sky will not be as happy an arrangement of form as it may be half an hour

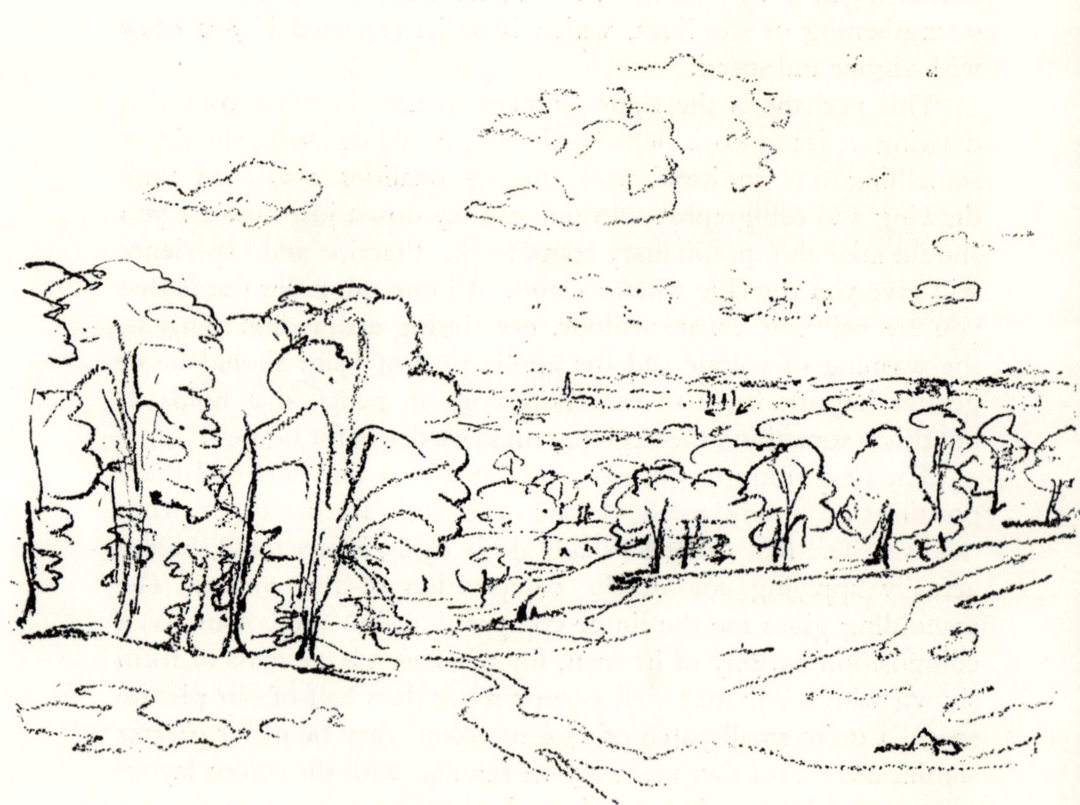

LANDSCAPE PAINTING: Stage One

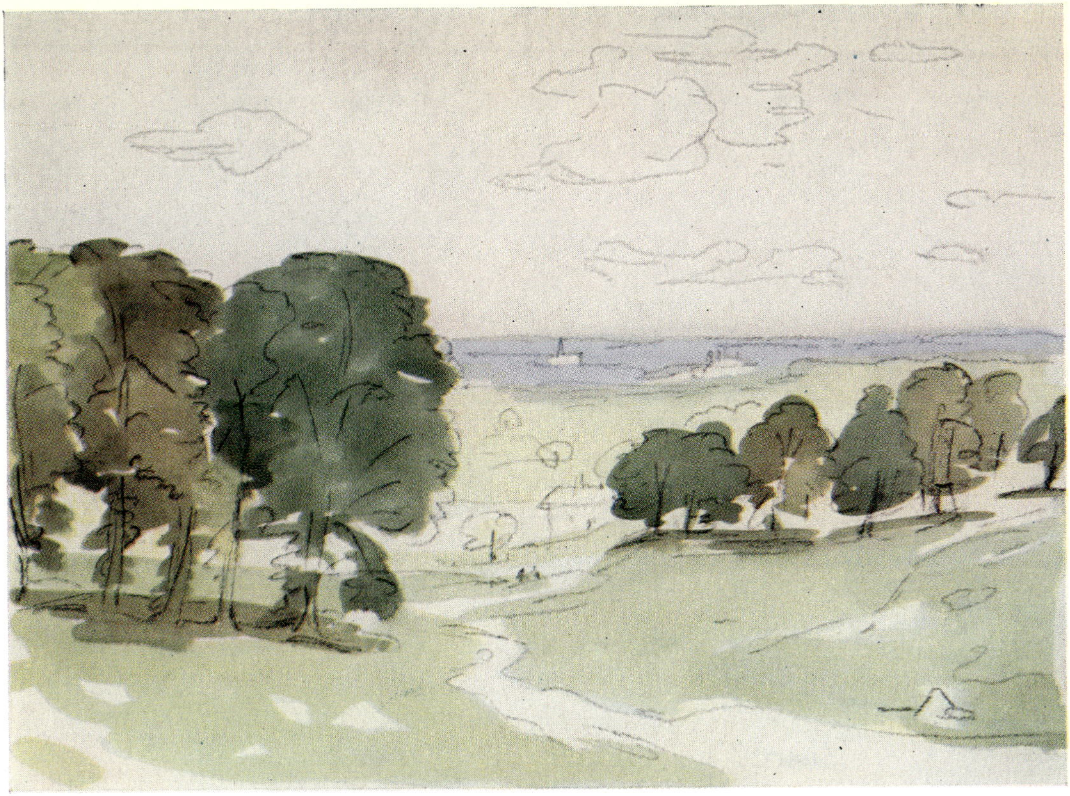

LANDSCAPE PAINTING: Stage Two

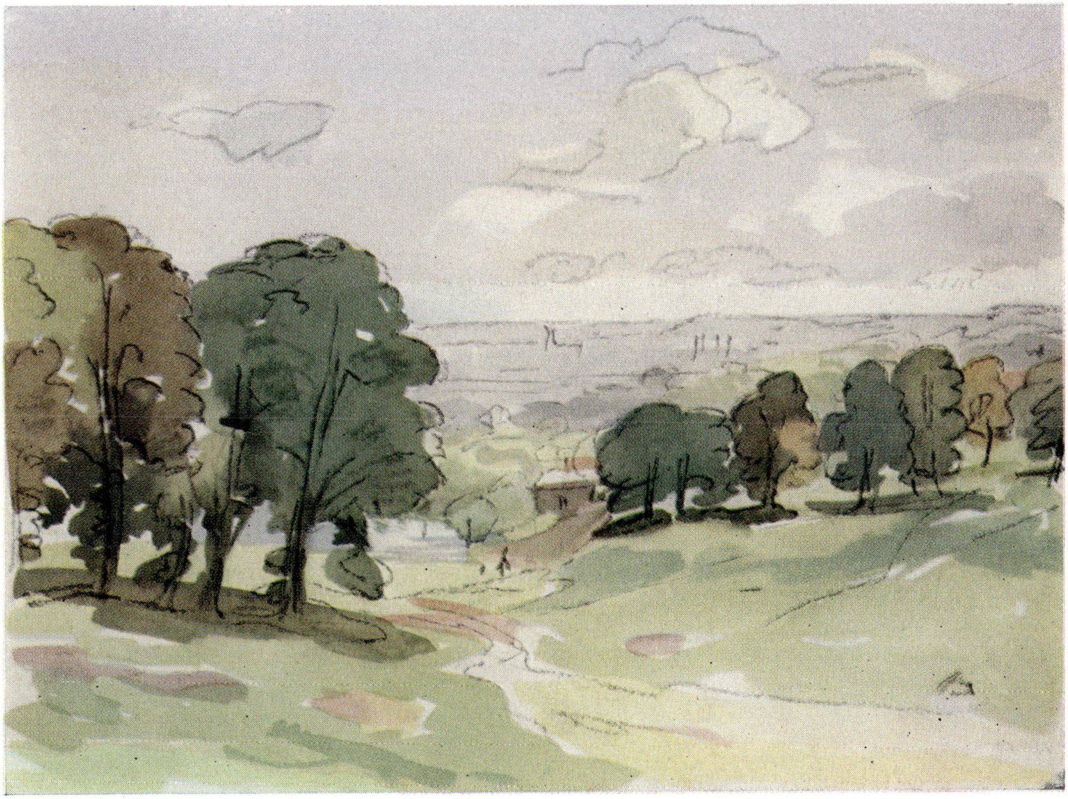

LANDSCAPE PAINTING: Stage Three

later. The cloud forms may, at any moment while you are actually working, present themselves in a lovely way. This is just when you should tackle them, and not just follow the habit of always beginning from the top and working down.

One of the very first things that I do, as far as the actual painting is concerned, is to mix up plenty of the main three colours I find in my composition. In this particular scene they are dark green, light green and blue. Starting with dark green for the group of trees to my left, I lay in a wash for the large areas (a) and (b). I use a fully loaded brush No. 14. Next a similar group to the right, using perhaps a little more water to my colour than before.

Back again to the next darkest green on the left. This green is slightly lighter and warmer in colour, therefore using some of the dark green just used, I drop a little more water into it while adding a little raw sienna or light red. Mixing it thoroughly I apply my full wash of colour to (c).

You will notice that these washes of my dark green carry on right down almost to the ground where the shadows, which are even darker, begin to form. But I don't want to put the shadows in yet before I've painted the grass on which the shadows of the trees lay. So the next problem is the foreground and middle-distance greens. The green is broken here and there by little bumps and hillocks, and patches of bare soil. So, paying attention only to the largest and most significant ones, I shall lay in my middle-distance greens, being careful to leave little bare patches of paper here and there, into which I will afterwards drop a little earth colour—yellow ochre or light burnt umber, to pull off this broken grass and earth, etc. (D) is considerably lighter than the greens of my trees to right, and left, and also a rather more yellowish green than the trees. So I mix up in one of my other pans a good amount of light yellowish green for (d) and lay it in from left to right, almost up to but not quite touching the edge of my dark green trees (a)—(b), unless of course (a)—(b) are dry.

If I touched into it while it was still wet, it would obviously run into my light green.

Next, using a little more raw sienna with this same green, I can float in my foreground, (e)—(e), either side of the path. This colour can go right across the dark trunks of the trees to the left. Don't worry about painting around them. Pass your brush right through them. You can pick them out with a dark colour over the green afterwards when the green is dry.

With all the largest areas painted in I can better judge the true tone and colour of the far distance. This is one reason for leaving it till last, because you will often find that should you paint it in at first rather than later in relation to its neighbouring colours, you may make too much of it in strength and tone. In consequence you will find that to bring the remainder of the picture up to it will require almost raw colour from the tube. This will of course defeat your plan to paint transparent and wet. Distance is a most deceptive problem, for if we isolate it from the foreground sky, etc., it invariably appears a very strong grey, blue or purple, but when judged with the sky and foreground you will notice how much greyer and paler it appears. And spotted in the distance are many other colours besides the general blue or grey. Roofs shine pearly-grey or red, or their shadow sides darker than the general blue colour of the distance. A splash or two of red or orange perhaps from roof or factory, or dark grey of church dome or chimney—all these will have to be added, either by painting over the general distance colour or by painting into the spaces I have left for them. Next back to the shadows of the trees, left, which are middle-blue with just a suspicion of grey or raw umber in the colour. These I lay in wherever I find them, linking the shadows on the trees themselves with the shadows on the ground as in my sketch.

Next the dark trunks themselves—a mixture of ultramarine and raw umber, bold and clear. Tracing the branches through the mass of foliage I pick them out with a smaller brush wherever I can find them.

Being a summer day I find that even the so-called whites of the clouds are warm and tinged with a little ochre or pink, so I shall wash my sky all over with a very pale colour, a mixture of ochre or sienna, with perhaps a touch of light red, very pale, of course, and with plenty of water. This tint I apply freely and with gusto, not caring whether small slips of white paper grin through here and there. This wash should not take long to dry, but one can always hurry the process by using a piece of blotting paper. The top half of my sky is clear blue, a mixture of Prussian and cobalt, with just a speck of light red in it. (The little red takes the rawness and newness out of the blue.)

The blue comes right down to the tops of the clouds to the right. Then it becomes paler and warmer, as it progresses down to the top of the far-distant clouds. Beyond this it is extremely pale and more mauve than blue. (This is obtained by adding more water with a little alizarine crimson.)

The shadows of the clouds are warm grey; so, with a little raw umber and black, with perhaps just a little blue, I can float them in wherever I find them, putting in the darker masses of cloud shadow first, and gradually diluting the colour with water as I work round to the lighter ones. The shadows of the distant clouds have been attained with raw umber.

Down now to the lane, in a light ochre colour, which one can wash in with a minimum of trouble, leaving the ruts and marks in its surface to be added either into the wet colour or later when dry.

All that remains to be done is to go over the ground once again checking up here and there, adding a detail where necessary, perhaps strengthening one that already exists, perhaps adding a figure or two or even a little black and tan dog somewhere—anything to give a touch of life to the scene. So many quite brilliant landscapes are marred by the absence of just that little touch of interest.

It may only be a puff of smoke from factory stack, or distant farmstead, or a brilliant white cotton-wool one from a passing train, a figure, or figures, or some animal, or a kite, bright red, yellow, floating in the sky. Little additions such as these will help to invest your painting with human interest, making it so much more interesting and enjoyable a work to look upon from the spectator's point of view.

Here, then, is a water-colour painting measuring no more than 12 in. by 15 in., which takes up about an hour, or an hour and a half, if you concentrate on the big shapes first. If you start the other way round, with the details, you will never finish.

A word on the handling of certain points in a landscape of this type. In painting the edges of trees, such as those on the left, where the contour of the green comes in contact with its surroundings, sky, distance, etc., notice how I have taken care, when laying the first dark green colour to give the contour some interest. The contour of the tree is broken up in some places and it almost looks as though little bits of the sky have crept into the tree, and vice versa.

This is managed at the start when laying the first washes. You can always add a little detail later when the colour is dry, such as a spray of foliage against the sky. The simple truth, and one that takes some time for the student to appreciate fully, is that a fresh wash of colour, whether for tree, foreground, roof or cloud, if handled well, will save endless trouble and explain ninety per cent of what you are trying to express.

So much for painting a view of this type. The student may well ask what happens when he is faced with a very different problem, such as a river, beach, mountain or forest scene. For instance, I think I can safely say that of all the very many problems with which the student is faced, the painting of water is certainly one of the most difficult. Possibly this is because water demands only the finest water-colour technique to capture its transparency and limpidity—the two essential qualities demanded of every true water-colourist.

Here again I might mention the reproductions of certain artists, contemporary and past, careful study of whose work will simplify much that is both complex and mystifying to the artist. Colour-photographs are also of value providing they are not touched up. Many of the details and characteristics of rivers, sea, foliage and architecture, can be studied at your leisure. To grasp such points when actually beside a river, is not always possible. By patient study of such sources of information, much can be learnt. Look at Turner and Constable, especially their sketches of river and seascape. Wilson Steer's seascapes will open your eyes to yet another way of tackling such problems in an even simpler tone. At any odd moment of the day you will be able to go back to check up and look over again your reproductions and photographs. You might even carry a few around in your pocket which you can examine at any odd moment. By such means you will become familiar with so very much of what can be found in nature but which eludes you when in nature's presence.

If your problem is running water, two of the best sources of information are the river scenes of Lamorna Birch and Munnings. The latter artist, especially, because you can see the same decisive handling of colour, tone and form for river, sky and landscape as in his better-known horse paintings. The general colour has been put in first and the texture or surface colour of the water added to that. The difficulty is, of course, that the whites of the water must be left white paper. Should you cover the water area completely in colour, then your whites or highlights, and foam, will have to be picked out, either by lifting with a sponge or brush, or by scraping when the colour is quite dry. (This is only possible when the paper is heavy and strong. Lightweight paper will not stand up to such treatment.)

Here I must mention that these two particular artists have produced very fine studies of running water but mostly in oil-colour, so you will only look to them for their handling of tone, colour and drawing. The transparency which we are after, i.e. the transparency of pure water-colour painting, can obviously not be found in either of the works of the two artists just mentioned. The water-colours of Sargent and Brabazon are also well worth looking at for their expert handling of water, river, foliage, old stone, etc. Look especially at Sargent's paintings of Venice. These are done in one go on the spot and are paintings of tremendous charm and vitality. If you are fortunate enough to come by suitable reproductions of these paintings of Sargent, they will well repay your attention.

Train your memory as much as you can because you will not always find nature willing to halt the passage of clouds or light and shadow across the landscape. You will have to paint with vigour and speed because she is ever ready to elude you.

Painting out of doors is rather like stealing apples from the orchard. You have to work fast and be sure of what you are doing or you will be caught . . . in our case, by nature changing her mood. One moment it will be calm, the next a wind comes up. Nature, it seems, is jealous of our humble attempts to capture something of her wonder and beauty. Skies can be extremely tricky at times, but not if you tackle the problem with a plan in mind. Development of your visual memory will greatly assist you to overcome any trouble caused by the sudden change of sky effects, such as the movement of clouds.

Decide where certain clouds are and, putting your sky colour in first, build them up with their shadow sides and light sides. Obviously, you cannot move your clouds once painted, so don't try. Even if you succeeded, the mess created would not compensate for the loss of freshness in the handling. Carry with you at all times if possible a little sketch-book, small enough to fit comfortably into a coat pocket or a handbag. Sketch everything of interest that comes your way. These jottings and ideas will give tremendous power and force to your work later on. Also, should you wish to paint a landscape in your flat or studio from memory, these bits of information will be of the greatest value to you.

Make sketches of barns, cottages, hills, rivers, old stonework, shrubbery, trees, doorways, windows, hay-carts, dogs, animals, children—in fact everything you possibly can. They will come in useful some time, probably when you least expect it. As sketches they may also possess some charm and value of their own.

HOW TO PAINT FLOWERS

FLOWERS have held the greatest fascination for artists for thousands of years, but not until the fourteenth century were they used primarily as a motive in painting, at least in picture painting. Up to that period they had only been used for decorative purposes—frieze and manuscript.

When the student pauses to look at the last five centuries of flower painting, he may well be at a complete loss to know just what school he should follow. From the great Dutchman, Van Huysan, to Chardin and Fantin Latour, there is such a wealth of variety and splendour of genious, that the choice is very difficult.

For many students flower painting conjures up great bouquets of peonies, chrysanthemums, even orchids, magnolias, convolvuluses and roses. Although the more expensive and exotic flowers are certainly the greatest pleasure to paint, my heart goes out to the humbler flowers to be found in hedgerows and country lanes, which are certainly as worthy of our consideration as the more expensive kinds in shops. For instance, the common daisy, white and yellow, the little yellow buttercups, daffodils and dahlias are really so lovely and so full of interest and even mystery, once one tries to unveil their form, that there is great expense and only little material advantage in attempting the more cultivated and exotic kinds.

No two flowers are alike, not even two Michaelmas daisies picked from the same spray, nor two buttercups from the same spot. Their character and individuality is the artist's problem, every bit as much as the established problems of tone, colour and form. Two small flowers that look very alike will be found to have many real differences once you begin to study them closely, seeking out their individuality of line, colour and form.

That is exactly what I would ask you to do when you come to paint flowers. Far too much paint is splashed around in the name of flower painting, which is full of the vaguest drawing and generalization. Wild throwing of paint will never capture anything in the visible world. No matter how excited the artist may feel, his head must be firm and cool fully to overcome the difficulties which are no more than in landscape painting but certainly demand more search and consideration. One reason for this is that when you are painting flowers, you are painting them comparatively near to you and in consequence you find them in sharp focus and in detail. In landscape painting on the other hand, only a relatively small amount of the picture space is occupied with anything as near to you as the bowl of flowers you are painting. I would recommend the beginner to study a single flower at first until he feels quite sure of himself in regard to the drawing of the flower itself. Choose a simple one such as the common daisy or buttercup. Select one with plenty of leaf and draw it again and again in various positions, turning it this way and that and also putting it in different lights. Get it one moment under a full light and the next away from it. Then lay it down on a table-top or book to study how the petals bend and fold under its weight. Count the petals and even separate one from another to see exactly their shape and form. All this you should do in your notebook or small sketch-book for these notes will come in handy later on.

Remember that if you can draw a flower well, you can draw anything.

Firstly, I would ask you to find yourself some good colour reproductions, just as you did for landscape painting. Choose reproductions of flower studies by Albrecht Dürer and the early Dutch masters, also Chardin, Fantin Latour and Chinese flower paintings.

My reason for adding Chinese flower paintings to the collection is simply that the brilliance and freshness of Chinese flower painting has never, to my knowledge, been equalled by any European artist, that is, at least in water-colour painting.

Where the background is concerned, it is best to keep it as simple as possible, certainly at first; and this also applies to foreground as well. Later on you may possibly be equipped to paint a mass of flowers against a most intricate background pattern, but for these first tries it would be most unwise. You will want your centrepiece, or motif, to be the flowers themselves and not the background, or the foreground; so keep them as quiet as you possibly can at first. Then after a few attempts gradually bring in a bright piece of cloth background, possibly red or terra-cotta, or blue, ultramarine or cobalt. In fact, whatever colour appeals to you, but which also appeals to you with the flowers upon it. The same change of material or colour can take place in your foreground. Start with a simple one, with no pattern at all, and from time to time change it for another.

The jug or vase into which you arrange your flowers should be of the humblest kind and the most simple in shape you can possibly find. One of the loveliest is of course the simple earthenware water or milk jug—Victorian, or earlier if possible. Earthenware jugs are to be preferred to so many other types for they possess all the qualities of importance—line, colour and shape, with little or no reflected light, being unglazed.

Also, because they are a simple earth colour and dull tin tone, they make a perfect foil for your bright flowers. You will want to take all manner of vases or jugs, from fairground prize to Chelsea lustre jugs, to hold your blooms—and so you should. You will experiment. Anything that appeals to you to use, you should use, whether you have to beg or borrow it. If you set your heart on a particular vase, or bowl, or jug, that you feel you must paint, get it by every means. Try to cut down as much as possible the use of china with fancy or fussy designs on it. The nearer to Delft the better. It is also a great delight to paint glass vases or jugs with flowers, especially so because you can chase the stems through the glass.

The petal forms are quite simple and the design of each flower easy for the student to grasp. White dahlias are another flower ideally suited to flower painting. As are Christmas roses—a most delicate and lovely white flower, with its dark green leaves in a bowl, the white flowers making a lovely pattern of stars on the dark ground.

Blossoms of pear tree and apple are certainly a "must" in any flower-painter's calendar. These can be pinned to an upright or placed in a vase. If you wish to paint a single spray, a very good idea is to fix it lightly, possibly with a pin here and there, to a sheet of ordinary cartridge paper, to be placed in an upright position. The sheet of paper can be fixed to the wall or wherever you find the light suitable. With light apple blossom, you should place it against a darker tone than itself—say a grey, brown or blue. This will help you to see the pattern more clearly which will in turn make the overall shape or silhouette of the blossom on the dark background less difficult to realise.

To tackle this exercise, I would suggest that you draw in carefully a spray of blossom, for example, as in sketch:

Pay particular attention to the outside edge of each flower, because only by serious attention to this edge, which is part of the silhouette of the flower, will you get the general character and feeling you are after. So much so is this true that if you leave the area for the blossom free, that is, painting up to its edge everywhere—but leaving the actual blossom clean paper—half of your task will have been accomplished. As far as seeing the silhouette of flower form, that is, getting the "feel" of the general pattern they make, try putting them before a strong light—sunlight if possible, if not, electric or candlelight are almost as good, but of course with the latter the edges are less distinct—and observe the shadows as they fall on to a white piece of material or paper. This is a little trick that one associates with silhouette portraits at the fair, on Hampstead Heath on a Bank Holiday, but its value goes far beyond giving a little amusement at the Fair. All through your working life, as an artist, whether student or professional, you will be concerned with the big shape first. And what better way to see this big shape but in a shadow where the detail within the contours is in shadow, and thus not hindering us.

Another tip is to hold a spray of blossom attached to cartridge paper against a strong light. The silhouette will come through the other side of the paper and appear as a shadowy version of the blossom's shape. This question of silhouette is far more important than most books on the study of art allow for. To the trained artist or draughtsman, the question of seeing the big shape first has been with him so long as to make him unaware in some cases that the student can not only do it, but—even more to the point—possibly understand what is meant by it. Remembering my own confusion as a student when faced with the cliché big shape, I can well understand the present-day student's reactions. That is why I offer these tips for seeing the overall shape or silhouette by using shadows. The most important thing is to learn what is meant by "the silhouette" or "large shape" first.

After shape comes form. Some shapes are identical with the form, such as a circle and sphere, square and cube, but they are only of the simplest forms. So many shapes one finds have little relation with the form, and in many cases utterly different forms are created within the overall shape! After having found the shape, your next problem is to search into the shape for its content or form.

The form of such flowers will be convex, others concave such as open tulips; while others will present flat or rounded forms, all of which should be observed and faithfully recorded.

Next to form comes colour, and this is perhaps what the student has been waiting for. The use of colour! Good painting dips deep and long into colour, but no more than it does into drawing, tone and composition. There are times when the colour runs away with us, a joy so difficult to harness at times: with mauve hydrangeas, red roses, or the yellow of sunflowers, marigolds bedded in dark green leaves, splashed here and there with yellow zinnias and large white daisies, or deep red roses with a yellow one or a pink one in their midst.

Such colours are hard to control or rather, I should say, such colours make it difficult to remember control. But one must exercise control with bright colours every bit as with soft or neutral ones.

Colour is possibly the most attractive of all the components that go to make up good painting, for everyone can visualize and appreciate colour (at least almost everyone), whereas few enthuse so wildly over drawing, form or tone. To primitive man, as to civilized man, colour excites us to joy, calm, gaiety and even melancholy. In short, its beauty is its great strength and weakness. The student so often fails to realize that good colour is not necessarily putting bold red and orange and green together, or yellow and violet side by side; but by careful balance of his palette, even when working predominantly in greys. You should try to remember that bright colours have grey in them, while greys have a great deal of colour in them, if only you search it out.

Therefore, when you are faced with bright colour which seems to shout at you, exert a steady hand when mixing the colour, for colour is always so very much more subtle than we think it is.

Next comes tone, which is every bit as important as form and colour. What do we mean by tone? By tone we mean the correct relationship of one colour to another. It is best explained by reducing our flower grey to black and white or monochromatic colouring. Imagine that you had a group of roses in a bowl. It is so much easier to visualize distance by the use of tone if we think of the exercise on landscape painting, for there the far blue hills are so very far away that the colour is pale compared with the dark trees on the left.

Imagine yourself standing on a red carpet that unrolls in front of you for miles right on to the far horizon. You will notice how the colour fades as it goes farther away from you, as a result of the atmosphere. Tonally, the colour at your feet would be of a certain strength while in the distance it would be much lighter in tone. This takes place in black and white just as it does in colour. If you had a black carpet at your feet going off into the distance to the far horizon it, too, would fade, the farther it went away from you. Thus, by the careful use of tone, you can explain perspective with your colour. In fact, you can think of tone as colour in perspective.

As far as the drawings of your flowers go, you can use charcoal as a change from pencil. This you can dust off (or most of it) leaving sufficient guide for the actual painting. You will want plenty of leaf round your flowers and this will help to link up flower with flower and serve as an excellent and restful foil to the colours of the flowers themselves. Look for the difference between one green and another; some will be yellowish while others, e.g. the green of carnation stems, can be quite cool and even acid in colour.

Later on you might draw your group in with a brush without using pencil or charcoal; this is a most enjoyable method and adds very much to the beauty of the finished effect.

For this you would not necessarily require such a small brush as you may think. A good sable would be ideal, providing it has a fine point. The colour to use for your drawing should not be too bright and certainly not too dark. Sepia or a little grey, with a touch of light red, is, I have always found, a most suitable colour. This you will dilute strongly with water, so that your drawing in will be pale yet fully explained and quite clear to see.

Water must be kept clean at all times. This is sometimes troublesome for the beginner to remember! For after quite a short spell of painting you will find the water getting dirty and muddy and this can add greatly to your difficulties if not checked in time.

Colours for flower painting should always be mixed from the main colours in your box and thinned to the required tone or strength with water. Do this rather than use off mixtures you may have had already mixed in your pan.

If possible, always mix your colours by using the minimum of colours from your box. The reason for this is twofold; first, by doing so you will ensure that your mixture is bright and clean; second, the ingredients that go into its making will be easier to remember should you have to mix the same colour again.

The value of the last point will be appreciated when you find yourself out of sufficient colour when half-way through a wash over a large area, such as background or foreground.

With the light colours of flowers, mauves, pale yellows and pinks, or pale blues, you must be especially careful in getting both the right colour and the correct tone. It is better to paint it in a little too light or pale, building it up later with more of the same colour, rather than paint too heavily in which case you would have to wash some of the colour off with a springy sable and clean water.

Do you paint flowers in first or background in first? Or both parts at the same time? Well, it depends on the group you have chosen to paint. Looking through your viewfinder your composition may have a great amount of background, or very little. Few flowers may fill the picture space in which case the amount of background seen will be small indeed. You would therefore paint your flowers first, and vice versa, if the amount of background is greater than the area occupied by the flowers.

When you paint up to your flowers don't leave a hard steely edge. This is poor technique because it destroys the softness of edges found in nature and especially in flowers. Try not to be too fussy in your application of washes, large or small. That is to say, don't fiddle about in small corners to complete the wash. Should you miss a bit of paper, don't worry. Leave it, providing it's not too large and noticeable.

If there are folds in the draperies, of background or foreground, casting a heavy shadow, don't wait until the background is dry before putting them in, but choose the moment when the colour underneath is neither too wet nor too dry. This is something you will find out and solve with a little practice. Much of the beauty of shadows, their characteristics of depth and softness and age, can be got while the colour into which we are painting them, is damp. This causes our shadow colour to blur at the edges. With practice you will find that you are able to paint in leaves, flower, stems, jug, etc., one after another without having to cut them again, or if you do, it will only be very little. But for the first couple of tries, attempt nothing so ambitious or tricky. Go about it as conscientiously as if you were building a wall for the first time, and you will then find that habit and method with your individuality will create a style, which will be your style. Don't try to force the pace. Be careful over the drawing first, then see to the colour and tone. If you stamp the drawing you will have to retrace your steps—sometimes an impossible and messy operation in this most delicate of all media.

In flower painting you will have to add to the original nine colours mentioned in the first chapter as they would not have sufficient range for the many strange and exotic colours one finds in flowers.

Your yellow, cadmium, is ideal for most purposes but it

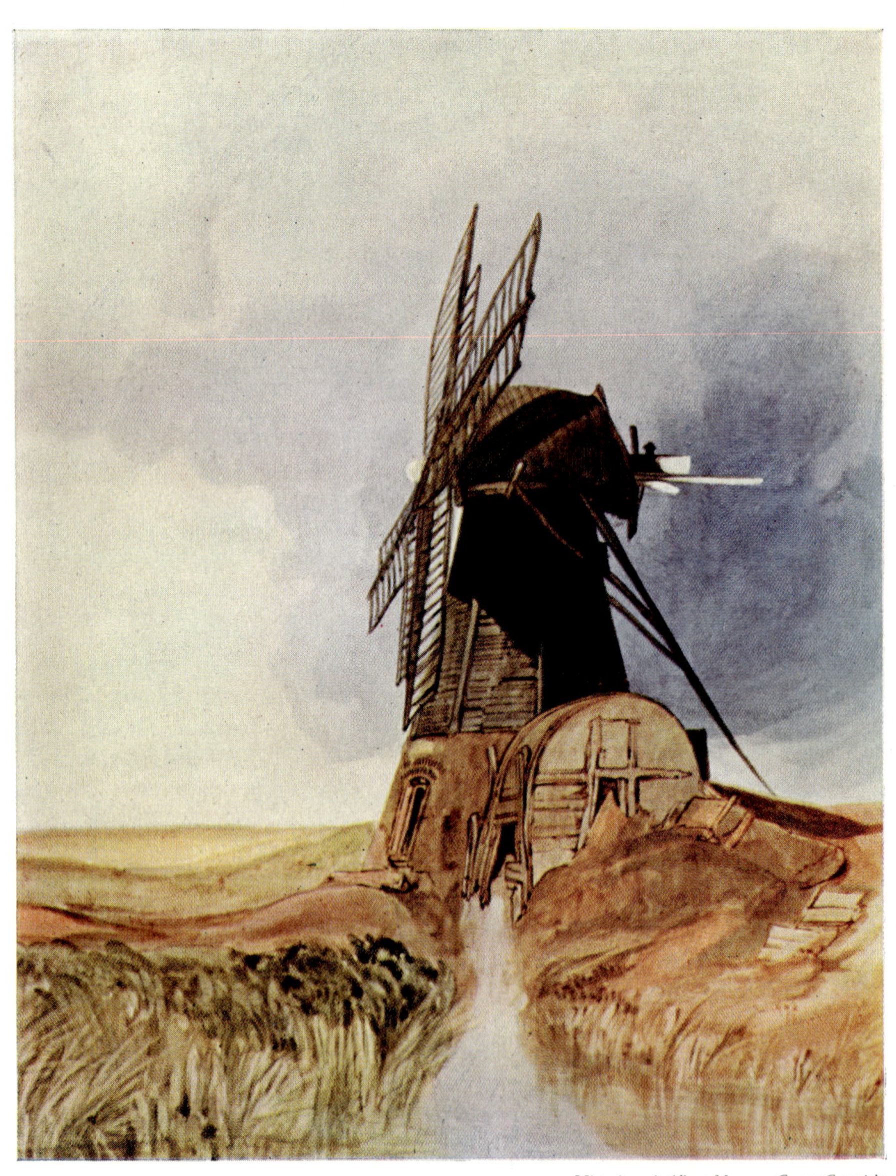

Victoria and Albert Museum, Crown Copyright

THE DRAINING MILL *by* J. S. COTMAN

might be found to be too yellow, or should I say, too hot a yellow, for some purposes, such as the palest daffodils and roses. So have a tube of lemon yellow handy just in case you should require it. Nothing is so exasperating as to be without the colours one needs.

Of the variety of reds, hot, burnt and wine reds that one has to contend with in painting flowers, vermilion and alizarine crimson will meet most purposes, but for the scarlet geranium and some of the more elusive shades of red for anemones, cyclamen, gloxina, etc.

This brings me to the deepest wine reds bordering on magenta and purple; for these you might find that the mixing of Prussian with alizarine crimson is not quite the rich colour you require, so have handy a little pan or tube of permanent magenta.

Cobalt and Prussian are your best possible choice for blues. But often one comes across a patch of sky or water where your cobalt or Prussian are found to be unsuitable, so have some ultramarine handy in your paint-box. So many of the blues one finds are very rich indeed and quite impossible to reach in intensity without ultramarine.

While on the question of Prussian blue, you should try experimenting by mixing purples with alizarine crimson, also raw sienna or yellow ochre. These will be found to be quite lovely and distinctive greens, rather autumnal in quality and often found when painting flowers, especially the leaves of cottage plants, gloxinia and geranium.

A word on keeping your blooms fresh might be of some value: some florists sell a little packet called "Floral Pack", which I believe is a great help in reviving flowers. Or you could use aspirin which is, from my own humble experience, a tremendous help once they are beginning to droop!

Remember that one of your greatest assets is your white paper. Once it is covered, it's covered for good or bad, and no amount of scrubbing out will ever quite equal the beauty of the untouched paper. When you come to paint the various parts in, be wise and exercise a little caution before barging in without thinking!

As far as the uses of brushes go, you will soon find that by discipline and practice, you will be able to do the most detailed and intricate work with quite a large brush such as a No. 10 sable. Besides, the experience gained by attempting to paint in with a large brush, even if you should not succeed at first, will not be wasted.

Treat your forms boldly. Be courageous, for success is denied the half-hearted in painting, as in most other things. So take the flowers that attract you—bright and brave mixture of blooms.

HOW TO PAINT A STILL-LIFE

FROM the moment you come indoors from the street you are surrounded on all sides by still-life objects in such variety and profusion that the selection of just what to paint becomes quite a task. The secret is in your collection of objects and your selection from them. To start from the beginning . . .

You all have a kitchen of pots and pans, earthenware dishes, carving knives, wooden spoons and other implements. Some people are proud possessors of copper kettles! Well, these are really the best possible articles to paint, and especially so for the beginner.

In many of the loveliest still-life paintings ever painted the entire "cast" has been chosen from vegetables, fruit, game and fish. The choice open to you is quite inexhaustible: from eggs, turnips, potatoes, shrimps. Remember that we appreciate paintings through our stomachs as well as our eyes, and those things that are a delight to eat are invariably a delight to paint.

Let us take, for example, the egg, immortalized in Velazquez' early studies of his family and friends in the kitchen. Who has ever painted eggs so faithfully yet so bravely? Or who has dared painting eggs being fried in a frying-pan since Velasquez' day?

I have mentioned this topic of eggs and Velasquez because

so many students are hidebound by convention and the times in which we live. They must be made aware by the example of the old masters, notably Rubens, Rembrandt and Velasquez, of the magnitude and range that is the painter's chosen domain.

Let us take a long look at Snyder's painting of fruit and flowers, fish and game, fully to appreciate the tremendous diversity of object, colour and form. Putting the clock forward 400 years we find that many of the basic ingredients for still-life painting in the sixteenth century are still used, while other objects such as newspapers and clocks, have joined the company.

Now let us take a few of these simple kitchen utensils and objects and see what we can do with them. Start with a bare table-top pushed up against the wall, with an earthenware or glazed pudding bowl and a wooden spoon dropped carelessly into it. Next, a red and white (or even a plain white) napkin dropped beside the bowl; a couple of eggs and a tomato or two would be sufficient to complete a group. Although comprised of a very few objects it would be quite satisfying from the painter's point of view. The wall might be pink or brown while the inside of the bowl and the eggs would be very light, making bright accents of colour amongst the darker tones of napkin and table-top. Add to this the shadow of the bowl on the table, and possibly a little on the wall, and the sharp shadow from eggs and napkin, and you have the makings of a most interesting group.

The important thing to remember is that your group should hang together. If you are taking things from the kitchen, such as a saucepan, napkin, egg, lemon, tomato and rhubarb, don't drop amongst them an oddity such as an old boot or a straw hat. Often students think that they have to buck up a composition by putting in a suggestion of whimsy. This is a fatal thing to do. If you are dealing with such objects, treat them seriously. This, of course, does not mean that you cannot bring a little humour into a group should you wish to do so. But it should be decidedly one thing or

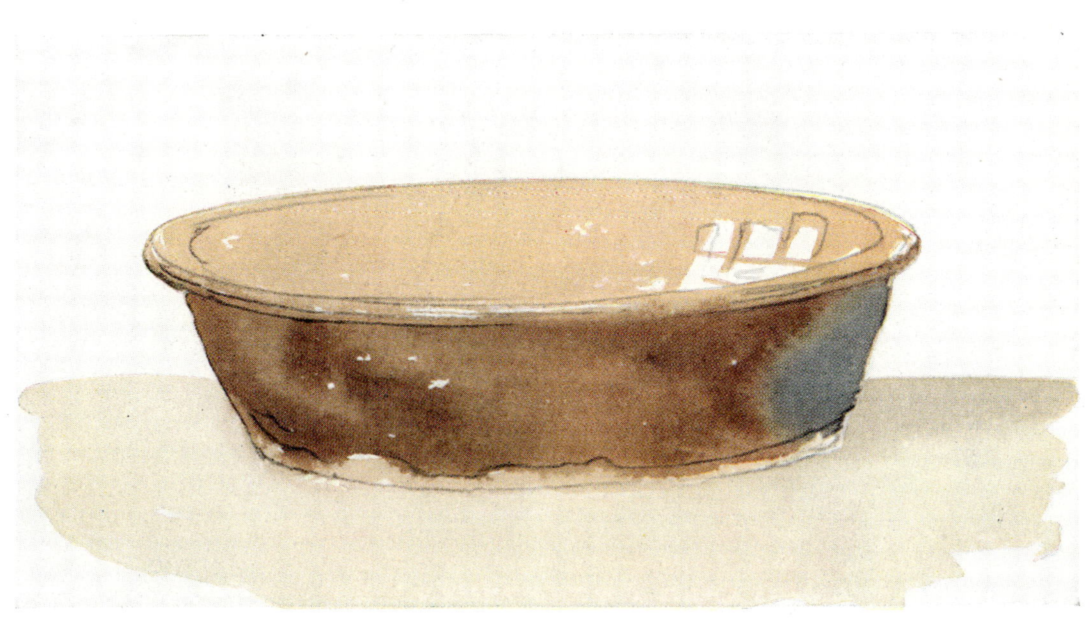

FIRST EXERCISE

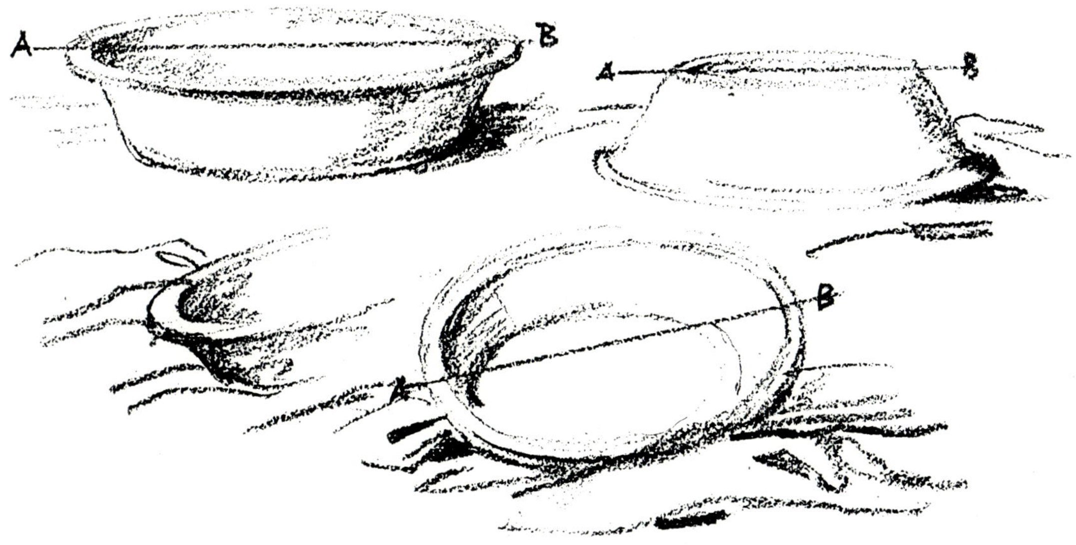

CHECK ELIPSES AS IN SKETCH

another, for the danger of falling into the trivial and superficial cannot be too strongly stressed.

Such objects as wooden salad bowls, cruets, mustard pots, lettuce leaves, lemons, with a few bright red radishes nestling in the green of spring lettuce and onion, make an ideal subject for the water-colourist. This is certainly more so for the beginner than pewter ware, or silver or copper pots. These are lovely things but one should have some experience first in painting non-shining surfaces.

Now for one or two simple exercises. The student would do well to take a single object first—a simple glazed baking dish, for example. Make yourself familiar with its form and shape. Its colour and tone will concern us when we come to put colour on to our framework. Place it in front of you and draw it as in sketch paying great attention to the ellipse and to the ends or sides of the ellipse, A-B. The loveliest colour will be for nought should the drawing be at fault. Check it, overall or depth, with the overall width A-B.

Next, tilt the object this way and that—possibly by placing a napkin or matchbox under one corner so that it tilts towards you. Again, look carefully for the ellipse A-B. If you feel that it swells as the line of the ellipse comes towards you, don't be worried, for in actual fact it does! But you must be careful to observe the ellipse closely to eliminate any distortion of its shape.

Look over the proportions very carefully, because accuracy here will help very much in getting the character of the object before you. Observe how the shadow from the dish links it to whatever it happens to be laying on! Once you are familiar with the proportions of the object by having drawn it, you can mix up plenty of the basic colour. This is usually a mixture of light red and raw sienna, possibly with a little raw umber to give it depth.

Mix plenty of this basic or general colour so that you have plenty to use for at least a couple of studies.

The dish should be placed on a white piece of cartridge paper with a light background. A quarter Imperial sheet folded in two would do admirably. Then you can use it for both foreground and background.

Float your general colour in over the whole of the lighter areas, as in Sketch A, being careful to leave the highlights clean paper.

Next, mix a little of your general colour with a darker colour such as raw umber or black for the shadow side of your dish. Test a little of the new colour next to the first wash applied to the dish. How does it go? Is it too light, or too dark? When you have the right colour, float it in, paying attention to any changes of colour such as an edge of reflected light, that you may find from the paper.

You can manage any reflected light in the shadow either by floating in your full shadow and then taking a moist brush and lightly taking off some of the colour applied; or you can break your general shadow colour at the edge of reflected light and then paint in the necessary colour with a fresh mixture.

Another way again is to float in your general shadow colour, first over the whole of the shadow area and then take some of the colour and depth out of the area occupied by the reflected light with a slip of clean blotting paper. This will considerably lighten the patch into which you will then drop your colour. Look for these reflected lights. They are invariably there even if sometimes they aren't too obvious. The use of them, once you have observed them, can greatly add to the quality and subtlety of your painting.

Remember also that too much reflected light is not a good thing, for it robs your group of the quality of daylight, in that it looks artificial as though it were an object on display, subject to more than one source of light.

On the light side of the dish where you have left the paper clean for your highlight you will need to go back perhaps and gently soften the edges of the highlights with a wet brush. Not all edges are soft, and especially so, with the highly reflective surfaces of objects such as pewter, silver and glass.

Again, not all parts of a highlight are necessarily sharp or soft. This is something you alone can watch out for, together with the particular type and pattern of highlight. For, as you know, what we vaguely term "highlight" is a reflection of some object such as sky or window. With the latter much interest can be got from close scrutiny and you will often be able to recognize the number of window-panes reflected.

Before I leave this matter of highlights I would ask the student always to check the relative tone or key of these highlights in relation to the general tone of the group, by having to hand a small piece of pure white card or paper to hold up in front of the group. More often than not, you will be surprised to find that the lightest light of your group is considerably less bright than your slip of white paper.

This method for checking tone can be used for colour also, at least for the first attempt. Colours such as blue, red, green, yellow and many others, but basically the primary colours, red, yellow and blue, are often very different to what you first think they are. In training your sight and appreciation of colour, this simple test is not to be ignored.

Get a colour chart from your art shop or interior decorator, and test yourself by first selecting certain colours in your group. Question yourself for the correct colour to be used from your box and then check it with the colour chart held alongside the colour in the group.

What happens if you make a complete mess of this first try? Put the painting under the tap, letting the water run over it. You might need to wipe gently with your sponge if the colour has become too hard and muddy. You will come away refreshed in spirit, armed with the knowledge that even when the painting is at its worst, you can always wash it out and start again. How the sculptor in wood and stone must envy the water-colourist his ability to do this!

Remember that freshly applied colour will wash out much cleaner than colour that has been muddied and worked over.

Over the surface of the dish you will most likely observe little variation of tone or colour, small marks or darkenings. Add these only after having laid in general colour and shadow side, when, providing you have worked with speed, you will find the colour still slightly moist. Into this you can add all the details that strike you as significant. In other words never attempt to paint more than you can see, and even then be selective!

Look for soft and hard edges; these are most important. Some objects will give a hard edge, or even a steely sharp edge, while others will be soft or even fuzzy. This is a point for the landscape painter in water-colour to remember, especially with distant mountains or hills, and, of course, skies! The edges of clouds are worth particular study in themselves. There is a whole world of beauty in edges; in their variety and loveliness. I well remember advice given me a few years ago by Sir Gerald Kelly, P.P.R.A., when speaking of edges: he said edges were things of great loveliness and we could only paint them well if we loved them.

Now take a last look at the dish before us. Is your study a full explanation of all you see before you? Look from the object to your painting again and again. What's wrong with the study? If it's weak in drawing it is too late to correct it, once you have applied full colour. But you can add a little here and there or take away, should you wish, with your clean brush. The result may be muddy unless you use clean water to moisten your brush.

So much for a simple kitchen dish. Now let us take a white china one, such as a deep serving dish—Staffordshire or Copeland ware, with figures, animals and landscapes in blue transfer upon them. Many kitchens have one. Even if the reader has not such an object I am sure he has some piece of white china with a transfer pattern upon it that will serve the purpose of this exercise just as well.

You will start in exactly the same way as you did the previous exercise, i.e. by placing the object in a strong light, and getting familiar with its proportions and the basic colour and tone of the white china. It may tend towards the ochre or grey type of white, or it may have a very slight bluish tinge to the glaze. After you have drawn the dish and given some indication of where the shadows fall from the object on to the table-top, moisten the paper with your sponge. You will look for the general colour of the china under the transfer first, and not the general colour of the dish when seen through half-closed eyes, which would add the colour of the transfer to it.

When you have tested a little of the colour on a bit of paper, judge what it looks like against the dish. If you are confident that you have the right colour and tone you should then prepare a quantity of this general colour, not only enough to paint on the pencil framework, but also a little extra. You will need some of this basic colour when you come to mix the shadow colour.

White china is rarely as white as you first believe it to be. It is usually much lower in tone than the highlights upon it. You have nothing in your paint-box to match the highlights, but you do have your white paper, so you will have to keep within this tonal compass, explaining with your paper all you see before you, from whitest whites or highlights, to the darkest dark, or even black. That beautiful off-white colour of the warm variety, you will probably get by mixing a little raw umber or yellow ochre with a dab of black. For the cooler off-white tints, take a little more of the black than yellow ochre, with perhaps just a little ultramarine added.

Before you float in the general colour, look carefully for the highlights, then shape and position, so that you can go around them with confidence, leaving a clean edge. If your paper is held at a right angle in front of you at about 45°, you will find that the colour flows down, making it an easy matter to glide the colour wherever you want it. If you are not quite sure about their position you will not get the right swing into your brushwork. It will look indecisive and messy in handling. When you have floated your colour in over the whole dish mix immediately your shadow colour. Perhaps a little raw umber or black in the last colour will be all that you need; but you will have continually to test your colour on a spare slip of paper to be sure you have it right.

Now float in your shadow, the large shadow first, gradually working round to the smaller ones. If the ground is too wet from the previous colour your shadows will float everywhere, so again you must look out and get familiar with this problem.

Don't hasten the drying with blotting paper. This should only be used for an emergency or if you deliberately intend to use it by floating in a darker colour than is really needed to begin with, to allow for the subsequent lightening of the colour by blotting. Once you have painted in your object, treating it as a simple off-white dish, then you can consider painting in the transfer upon it. The rendering of the pattern should be painted clean, and by that I mean that the very greatest care should be taken not to fuss over the pattern. You can indicate lightly the position of the main shapes with pencil first, and then with a well-mixed colour (for whatever the design is—blue, grey or sepia). Float in the general colour for the light area. As you work round to the shadow side you will require a little more strength to darken your colour. If the highlight comes across the design of foliage or mountain, you will have to allow for this and use a much diluted colour indicating the continuation of the design in the palest tint across the highlight.

As you float in this or that piece of detail, you will often find that when you lift your brush away from the paper the colour behind will create a little pool of strong colour. If you are using a large brush full of colour, this can be a nuisance; but otherwise it rather adds to the charm of water-colour painting. It can help to create that "accidental" quality which can add so much to the beauty of water-colour painting. So unless the pools of colour are disruptive to the desired effect, don't worry unduly about them. But if they are disruptive and troubling you, a clean brush will soak the colour up.

Remember that the design is something superimposed upon the dish, either by painting or transfer, and that it does not project in any way from the surface of the object. It lies on it and follows its form in all directions, never appearing to jump off the surface or sink beneath it. This is something which can be the greatest joy to pull off and the greatest credit to the painter.

As form goes away from you to left and right around the sides of the dish you must be as accurate as you possibly can to see that the pattern does likewise. A No. 6 or No. 7 sable is a good size to manage most detail with and the larger shapes can often be painted in with a much larger brush, such as a No. 10 or No. 12.

If the pattern is blue, you might have to experiment a while until you are satisfied that you have the right shade. Often the blue of china is an elusive colour and hard to mix. If your blue is hard and metallic-looking, try a touch of raw umber in it; or sometimes a speck of alizarine crimson will do the trick just to take the rawness out of your colour.

Should the transfer be sepia, that is, of the light red variety, you may find that it is tricky to get your mixed colour to match that of the original. If you have used light red and raw umber as your basic colours, you may find that a touch of blue with the light red is necessary. Often it is the complementary colour, such as mauve for yellow, or green for red, that will be the particular colour necessary to match the colour in life.

If the dish is the uncovered type with a patterned lid, and handle or knob, you will have to repeat the design and transfer on a convex shape and you will have to observe carefully just where highlights and shadows fall. If it is without a lid, you should look for the exact placing of the highlight in relation to those on the outside of the dish.

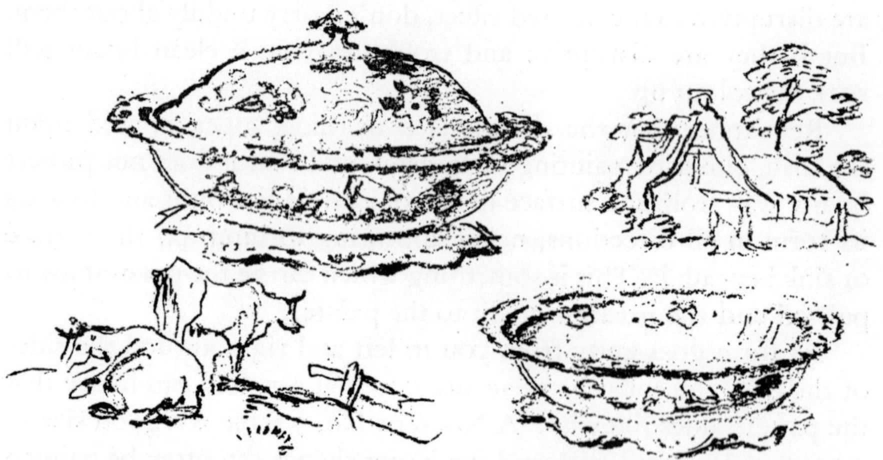

If you look at Velasquez, Chardin, Manet, Cézanne, Monet and William Nicholson, and many others, you will see, as it were, a thread of similarity running through one artist to another. They all painted kitchenware and made of it something wonderful to behold. You will never find trashy objects in any of their work, but those objects which, by their daily use, are of importance to their lives. There is a certain importance and nobility to the simplest objects used by their hands, especially those connected with cooking.

Now let us set up a full group of fruit and china with perhaps a gay-coloured napkin. Here some of the fruit can be arranged with pears and apples upon a red and white checkered napkin set upon a plain tablecloth. See my sketch for the sort of group I have in mind. Nothing very complicated and nothing expensive or rare.

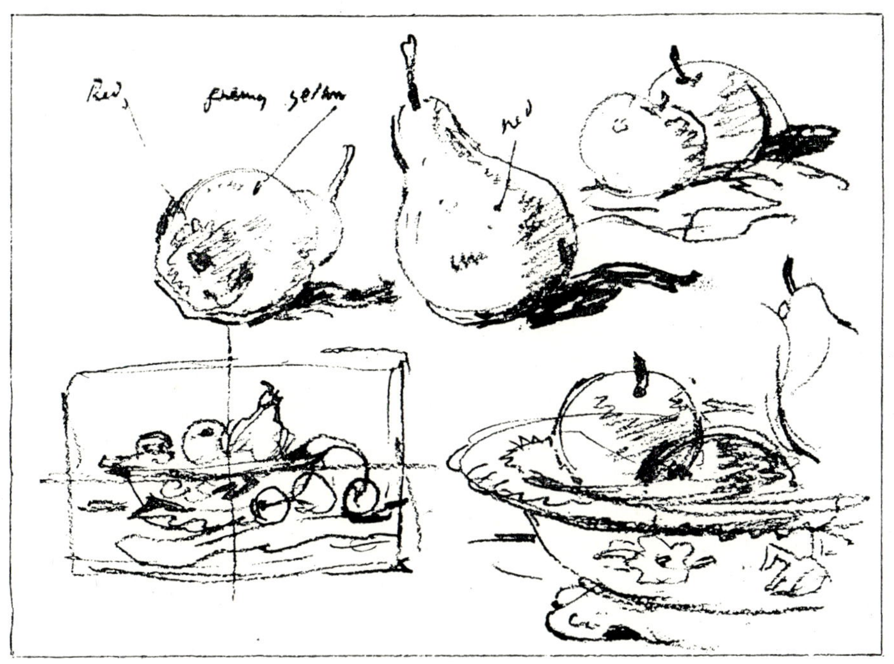

Studies for Still Life Group

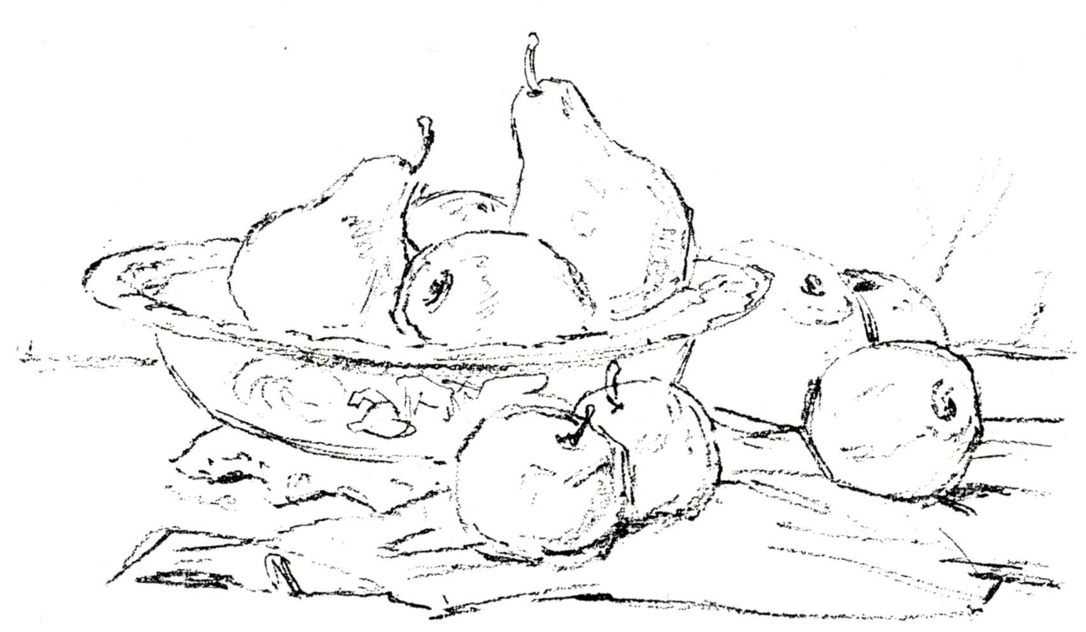

STILL LIFE: Stage One

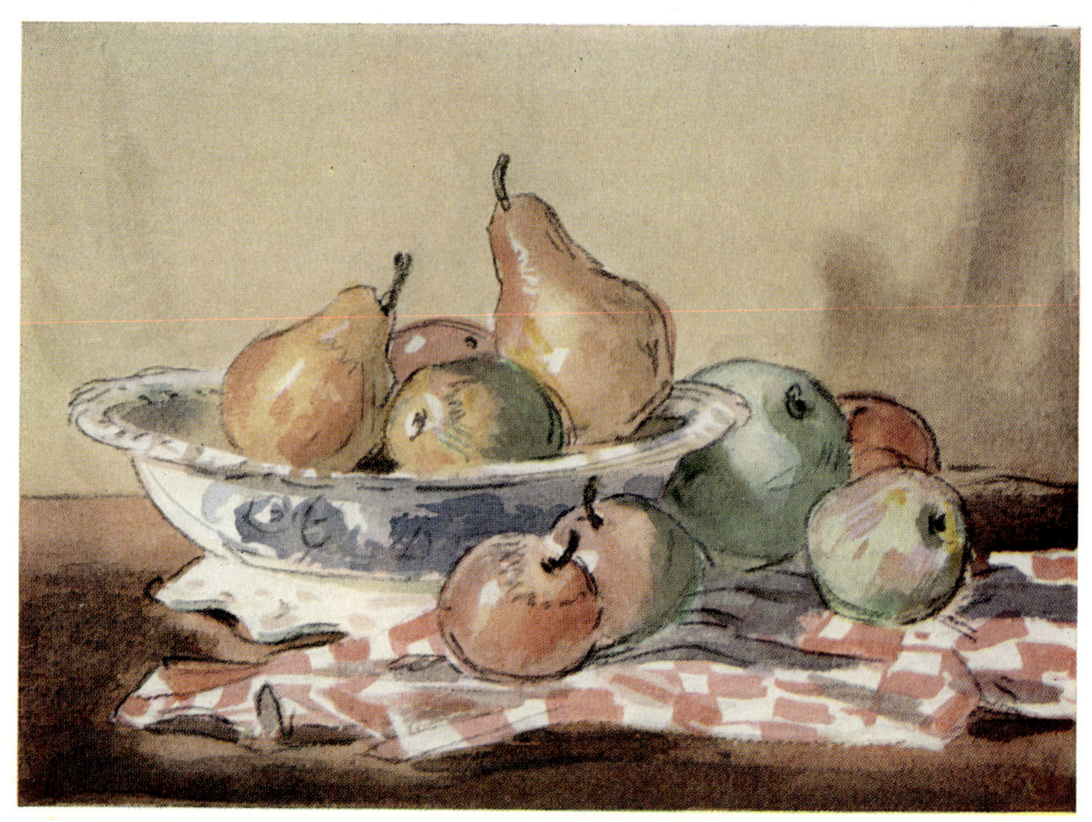

STILL LIFE: Final Stage

The blue dish has been charged with pears and apples upon a red and white checkered napkin set upon a plain tablecloth.

The apples and pears you paint you will choose yourself from the greengrocer's. Tell them you want to paint them and invariably they will let you pick them yourself. Choose those with lots of colour—the largest you can find—it doesn't matter how irregular in shape they are. A few specks add rather than detract from their loveliness. In my group I have one large cooking apple among the smaller eating apples. It adds distinction and variety to the group by its size and slightly acid colour. The common cooking apple is certainly one of the loveliest apples to paint and I have found that they stay fresh longer than eating apples.

The light should either be left or right, and the stronger the better. If the light is weak then the forms are weak and shallow, whereas if the light is strong you can grasp the point of the most subtle graduation of form and plane far better and with a minimum of searching.

The light comes from the left in our illustration and is strong, for I have set the table very near the open window. You will experiment in this way to your joy and advantage, for some groups are suited to a stronger or more direct light than others, while some of the best results can be obtained by using a suffused or indirect light.

Four or five apples are grouped on the napkin and I have taken care not to pose them, not to be too self-conscious over the placing of them. I have attempted to make them appear natural and accidental rather than arranged specially for picture making. The napkin is the simple red and white check sort which presents a pretty little problem for the student to paint, but a most colourful and gay one, if successful.

Now, as in the chapter on landscape, I would invite you to follow me stage by stage in tackling this group. A quarter Imperial sheet of Whatman (or heavy cartridge paper would do as well) about 200 Nott surface.

First I shall make use of two little sketches in my notebook, about the dish, the apple and, possibly, about the composition as a whole. By making little notes on individual parts of the group, I become intimate with the problem before me and thus more courageous about the actual painting. (See sketches.)

I damp the paper all over, and then, when nearly dry, that is, when the shine has gone, I draw my main forms using a piece of soft charcoal. From top to bottom, I now fix the position of the table against the wall, not too centrally on my paper, and then the slow pyramid made by the dish and fruit, reaching its apex with the large red and yellow pear to the left of centre. The line made by the edge of the napkin comes across almost the whole of the composition, leaving only a small patch of table between it and the bottom edge of the picture.

Wherever I have seen an ascent, whether of shadow or texture, I have given a little more weight to my scaffolding, all helping towards the actual painting. Perhaps I should mention here that this scaffolding in charcoal can be quite firm and sure. If it is too heavy you can always gently dust or flock it before laying on your colour. The charcoal line is usually broad and when flocked harmonizes beautifully with the subsequent painting in water-colour. A thin pencil line can look wiry and thin in comparison, though it is better suited to certain forms of water-colour painting such as architecture.

I then seek out in my mind's eye the lightest parts of my group, at the same time noting the position of the darks and half-tones. One has to be so careful about preserving the lights wherever they may be. I see that the lightest spots of colour in the group are the highlights and china of the dish, and the whites of the check napkin. Background, foreground, fruit, etc., are all considerably darker, while the composition of darks is quite thin and confined to shadows of fruit and dish, and a few folds in the napkin. The largest patch of clear colour I have is the background, and next to that the foreground. The background is a soft buff in colour, not dark, but dark enough to make the whites of the dish almost sing as they touch each other. So I carefully lay a wash over the whole of the background, and where the wash thickens here and there, I glide it round the contours of the fruit. I lightly pick off with a dry brush any little concentration of colour that I feel is disruptive of the desired effect.

The next large area of painting even colour is the foreground. As it actually touches the last wash to the left of the fruit dish, I can go straight ahead and lay it in. If it were not actually touching it, I would tackle something that was! The reason is simple enough. Colour can only be accurately judged when related to its neighbour, so that to paint odd parts of one's painting unrelated to the neighbouring colour, is a very random and risky practice. However well it may come off it will none the less be the result of chance and is not to be recommended as a method for beginners.

Each colour in turn must be judged in relation to its neighbouring colour, and so on in turn until your painting is complete. Then, of course, you can return to odd parts of the painting, to alter or add as much as you feel is necessary.

The table-top in the foreground was a raw sienna-like colour, though a little darker than pure raw sienna itself, so I add a little raw umber to it and just a dab or two of light red, to give it punch. Having floated this colour in over the whole of the foreground, I notice that the edge of the napkin is reflected into the surface of the table-top, and also a little reflection of the dish can be seen likewise. I can get the effect by picking off some of my foreground colour with a clean, moist brush to lighten it slightly. There is no particular order of work, as far as one part of a picture goes, apart from the point already mentioned about judging one colour in relation to its neighbour. But now that I have enclosed my fruit and napkin, with colour below and above them, I can choose anything I like to paint, so I shall start by tackling the blue and white fruit dish. This I carry through much as I have explained earlier on in this chapter with a similar type of dish. But in this group I see only about two-thirds of it, the rest being obscured by fruit, both in and outside. And, of course, the folds of the napkin cover the lower part of it. A small amount of warm green is reflected from the apple in the right-hand side of the dish, and although it is slight, I consider it worth putting in. This is done simply by mixing a little of the green and fusing it with the shadow colour on that side of the dish.

Now for the large green cooking apple—a very bright and intense green, although rather acid in colour. A mixture of cadmium with ultramarine I find unsuitable, as the blue is not strong enough to give me the acid green I'm searching for. So I try again with a little Prussian blue and find that it gives me exactly what I require. First I float my green, which is the general colour of the apple on the light side (about two-thirds of the whole area!) up to the shadow area. Then I quickly mix the colour necessary, using some of the green just used with raw umber and a touch of Prussian blue. Float in the shadow side with this mixture, starting where the light green finishes. As the areas of colour are wet, I find that the edge between them blurs very well which is exactly what is desired. Any little reflections in this shadow colour can be got by lifting with a clean, moist brush and then dropping the required colour of the reflection into it. The edge of the apple, as it comes up against the colour of the background may be a little hard. So I carefully touch around the edge with a well-moistened clean brush which just softens enough to make the apple contour fade away as it does in life. If your edges are hard, your eye will be dragged to them, whereas the "content" is what your eye beholds in nature, not the "contour".

For the painting of the pips or stalks it is not necessary for the colour underneath to be wet. In fact, painting such details in on a dry ground is an advantage as it allows greater freedom with less danger of blurring. For such details a clean dry edge is certainly better than a furry one.

I shall therefore leave such details until later. The next thing to occupy me is the painting of the two apples to the right. These are not unlike the colour of the cooking apple, though they are certainly darker and perhaps a little richer in colour. This is a habit of work I have got into—to work on whatever is the nearest colour to the colour just used. In this way there is less time spent in mixing afresh the colour required, because the previous colour can be used as a base.

Having painted in the two green apples in much the same way as I did the large cooking apple, I then proceed to paint the red apples and pears. I mix a reddish colour for the light sides, and am careful to leave those places to be painted in later where the yellow or ochre or green peel colour is decidedly different from the general colour.

The highlights on these reddish apples can be got by lifting the general colour off with a dry brush—while it is wet, of course. The shadow colour was floated in before the general colour on the left side had quite dried, just as I did with the large cooking apple. The pears present a very special delight because their shape and form is rather more subtle than the apple. The base is certainly similar to the apple, but then the form narrows, especially so with the Formichi pears I have used. I found that there were rather flattish planes to the waist and the top. Also, not all of them were evenly balanced. Some were heavier one side than another. Actually, this occurs with the apple, but it was less noticeable.

Where reddish streaks of colour come over the general yellow or greenish ground colour I painted them straight on to the ground colour. In most cases, I did this before the ground colour was completely dry. Thus the soft edges were realized simply by painting into wet.

The next thing was the napkin. I painted in the heaviest folds and shadows first. When these were practically dry, I mixed a clean amount of vermilion (with just a touch of blue to give it quality) and painted the squares in, the more obvious and simplest ones first, gradually whittling the problem down until only the squares or bits of square in the shadow or folds remained. These required a touch more blue to the colour. These I painted in, not troubling to give a razor edge to each piece of colour, but simply painting them freely. For the very best effect I might have gently moistened the shadows first, and then painted in the pattern of squares. The slightly blurred effect peculiar to the quality of shadows would have been even better achieved.

Lastly, I went over the painting from stem to stern so to speak, pulling little things together, adding details or improvements wherever I felt the need, finishing up with the sharp and deep shadow under the napkin on the table.

Here, then, is a typical and not very difficult subject for the student in water-colour. Much that I have mentioned, such as the softening of edges and the melting together of colours can be omitted should the student desire to pursue a more direct manner. In this case the finer points of technique can be cut down to a minimum; one can adopt a hit or miss method, depending purely on the attractiveness of colour.

The student should not be put off painting whatever appeals to him. Although some objects add to our progress and study, others are hardly worthy of serious study and can be of little or no value to us. Pewterware and brass, copper, kettles and pans are delightful things to contemplate. But they so often defeat the student simply because his eyes are full of all the reflections and highlights, at the expense of form.

After some practice with simple objects I would recommend

the student to tackle a pewter or silver-type tankard. Take it just by itself—as an exercise in itself. If you like, you can make of it a centrepiece for a group. But to use it simply as a means of study by itself is of greater use and, for myself, of greater pleasure! Stand it on a red book, and then move it to a white tablecover. Look for the shapes reflected in its surface. Turn it on its side this way and that, so that you can see the deep shadow inside it and under it. See how the shadow links up with the object itself.

Books are another thing you should practise with as much as you can. I well remember that one of the earliest exercises I made as a young student was a collection of old books, dog-eared and leather-bound, some of them with the leather spine missing or at best torn. An open book can be a great source of interest to the painter and a never-ending subject for observation and the polishing of your water-colour technique. Look at the changes from warm to cool as the pages open! Tackle the pages of lettering by judging carefully the general tone and colour of the print, rather than attempt to write the page in water-colour word for word. Unless of course you find a large letter or heading which by its size can be comfortably managed.

Vegetables, especially turnips, celery, swedes and spring carrots, are especially good to paint. The colours of rhubarb have inspired many a water-colourist and will no doubt continue to do so. The range of colour in this one vegetable from bright green through creamy white to the brightest crimson or cerise is a sheer delight to the colourist in any medium.

Another delicious thing to paint is the mushroom, especially when turned out of the bag on to the table-top or plate, so that you can see their dark brown undersides.

Pomegranates have always held a fascination for the artist, from Pompeiian times to our own. The slightly flattish planes on the outside, together with the colour and the shape of the stalk and leaf, give it a unique quality which make it irresistible to the painter.

These suggestions on what and how to paint are but a selection from a horde of possibilities. But I hope a few of the essentials have been put across to assist the student through his early attempts at still-life in water-colour.

FIGURE PAINTING

WHAT is figure painting? By this I mean costume painting to begin with and then groups of figures such as you would find in the market or on the beach or at the fair. The reader will now have some idea how to paint such subjects or to do a portrait in water-colour.

I have omitted the subject of nudes in water-colour as being outside the scope of this book. Present-day taste does not fancy painting the nude in water-colour, whereas groups in costume are the chosen subject of many artists.

Your small notebook or sketch-book is invaluable if you wish to master the characteristics of groups of figures. Make notes whenever you can and wherever you can, as swiftly as you can. This is an exacting test of your powers as a draughtsman, but unless you do sketch quickly it is possible that the figure or groups of figures may move.

Let us take the single figure first. A friend may well be kind enough to pose for you. Sometimes it is possible to find them without enlisting their help—as when you find a member of the family asleep perhaps with the newspaper over his head in a deck-chair, or simply having a quiet nap after lunch. Sketch in the main shapes first—much as you did with landscapes and still-life. When you have added scaffolding to the figure you can start laying in the big shapes. One method that you might like to try is to block in the diluted sepia colour—using perhaps a No. 6 brush very lightly—fixing with a little mark here and there where the head comes in relation to the shoulders—then placing the feet right in relation to the rest. A little mark is quite enough when using this very light colour. But be sure you have the character of the pose before you apply the colour.

Another excellent practice is to block in the figure first with sepia—treating the whole problem as a sepia monochrome—but not heavily! Once you have established where your shadows come and have painted them in—plus any other darks—such as a dark jersey or tie or shirt, together with the shadows on the shadow side of the figure—you can proceed to float your colour in wherever you find it. The beauty and value of this method becomes apparent immediately you apply the colour, for then you will find how easily your colours knit together.

The sepia lay-in will give not only a frame in which to place your colour but will help to give unity to your painting once the colour has been applied. This problem of unity is most important. You might also find this method most useful in figure painting, especially the single figure. With groups of half a dozen figures unity is also important but less in reference to the individuals than to the figures as a group.

If you are fortunate enough to find a friend or member of your family ready to pose for you, take advantage of your luck, and, if possible, really pose them. A standing pose can be difficult for a person not used to it. But there is a wealth of beauty and interest in the seated or reclining figure. Reading at a table or with a book in the lap is an easy pose to keep: the model can keep his interest alive by actually reading the book! Figure painting (dealing here with costume figure painting) is a most rewarding form of painting, for it can lead the student should he become proficient at it, into the ranks of the magazine and book illustrators. Apart from being a most interesting and enjoyable form of work, this can often lead to as much profit as pleasure. There is a tremendous demand for figure drawing in illustration and magazine work. Here I have in mind mainly the student who has decided to embark on commercial art. For him study of magazine illustrations is essential.

But for the person interested solely in the fine art possibilities of figure work—or looks on it as a pastime—I would rather recommend them to seek out the work of Boudin and study his perfect little water-colours of women and children, their hoop skirts blown by the breeze of the sea enjoying a stroll along the sands or on the promenade at Deauville. Observe how he has created the illusion of space and air around his little groups. Observe, too, how he has knitted together the knots of people into the unity we find in life. He is also able to create the feeling of a group and sometimes a small crowd with the greatest simplicity of means—a figure here, another there, two together, the head of another between them, and all composed so naturally. And in those lovely little blobs of colour, liquid and fresh, spontaneous and untickled, lie the wonder and the beauty of Boudin's work. If you look at a Boudin through a magnifying glass you will see what I mean. There is fire in every mark—the result of decision and speed. Your first attempts will not always have decision and often if they do, your decision may be a poor one or misplaced. But take heart from this, and learn more about yourself by opening your eyes to your weaknesses. When you feel you have the brush in the right spot, then be bold. The reverse is fatal, for to dither with the brush will only fog and muddle your work.

Do not attempt to paint eyes, noses, fingers, etc., in too great detail. Remember that if you are painting a figure three or four inches high on your paper it will be something like eighteen times less than life size. This reduction will make the drawing of such detail not only difficult but often unnecessary. A good suggestion is sometimes better than a more finished rendering. If you are

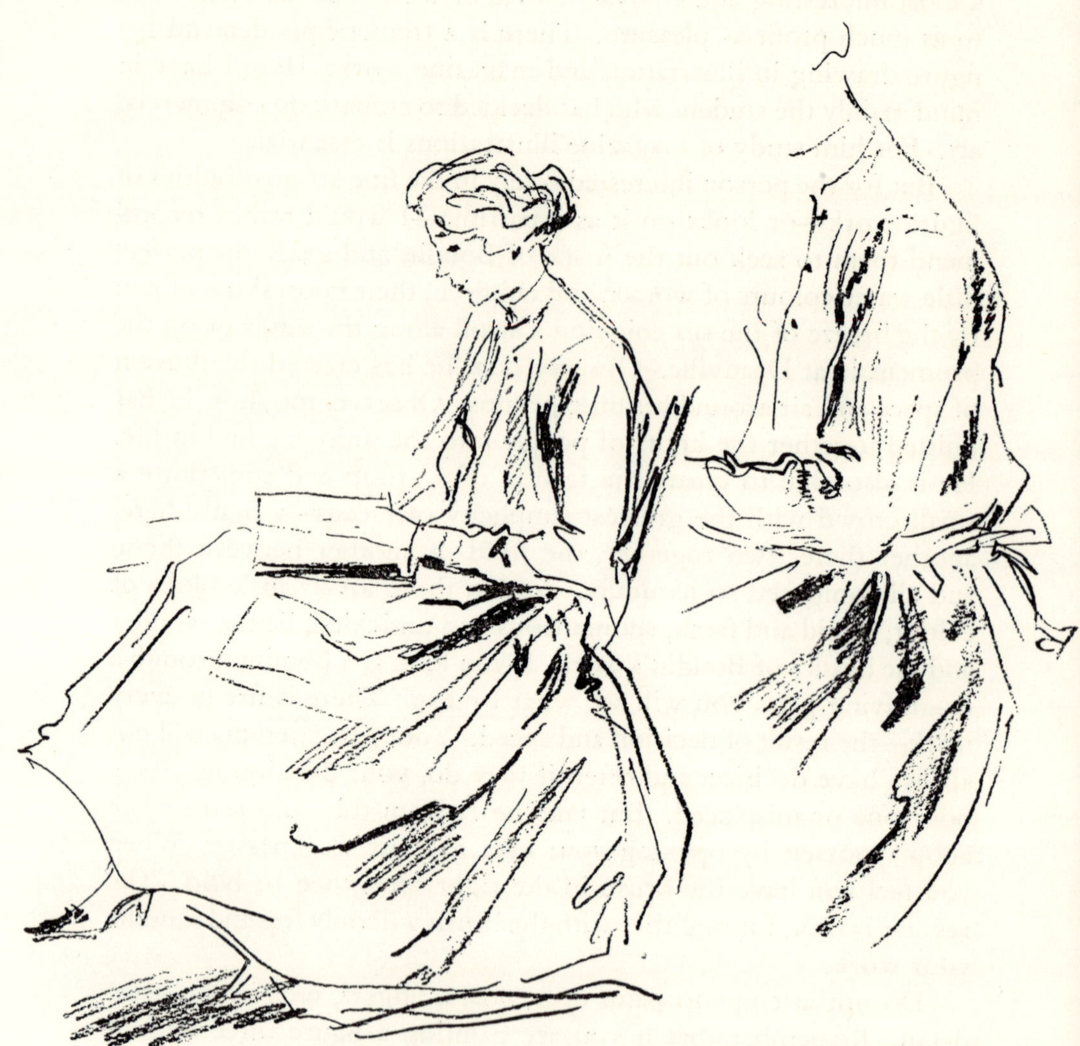

STUDY FOR FIGURE WORK

working on a very small scale—painting figures down the street or a hundred yards away on the beach—you obviously cannot be concerned with eyebrows or fingers but simply with their shapes. You should be as accurate as you possibly can over the shapes but do not embroider them with what your mind tells you, only paint what your eyes can see without too much straining. When painting objects, figures or forms near to you there is every good reason sometimes to look long and hard, in search of the truth you are seeking but which may escape you if you only glance at it. But with figures and forms far away from you it is best, I have found, to let them be and not to bring them too much into focus by searching for more than you can really see. The folds of material are often a trouble if you look for the fold alone and not for its direction. Look for the start of the fold and then you will lay it in with better conviction.

Look also for the quality of folds and creases in material of widely different character. The sharp lightning flash of satin and silks, the soft ones of velvet, and the handsome large folds of corduroy and leather. Many of these points are of course questions of draughtsmanship. But the problem of how it is best to tackle them is simpler for a brush than for a pencil or pen, because the brush can be wielded to give the thick one end and the thin the other end of the fold by simply adding or lightening the pressure on the brush. The folds in my sketch have been painted in this way, most of them in one stroke.

Should your figure be near you will want to pay attention to very many details of drawing and colour. For instance, if you are painting a friend no more than six feet away from you, seated perhaps at a table, head in hands with a book or tea things in front of him, you would wish to paint details such as the lights in the hair or on the shoes or the glitter of a wrist-watch your friend may be wearing. You would therefore have to be far more careful with your framework or scaffolding to ensure that there would later be no great fumbling in either finding room for these things or altering the position of them once you have painted them in. In this case I would suggest that you draw your figure rather carefully, first in pencil or charcoal. When you are happy about the drawing side of it you can then take the figure, piece by piece, in colour.

As with the previous exercise, you will find it better to start with the largest patches of colour first. What happens should the material be checkered or heavily patterned in some bright design? In that case you would go for the dark first adding your lighter colours when this is dry or almost dry. If the pattern is extremely complicated you might wish to draw it in first with some care. And if the pattern or design is fussy, then simplify it as much as you can, otherwise it may cause some irritation to the general effect of the finished water-colour.

The softening of edges and many of the other tricks one would normally apply in landscape are most necessary if you wish to execute a good rendering of the model. Especially when you come to the softening of the forms in the face of shoulders. This I have dealt with more fully in the portrait painting section of this chapter.

One of the loveliest and most exciting things you can possibly do, is fitting a figure into its surroundings. The secret is in thinking of the figure as part of its surroundings, at least, those things immediately around it. A common fault is to consider the figure alone, unrelated to what it is leaning on or sitting on or near, until the figure is finished and *then* attempting to house it in its surroundings. This is wrong—and leads to all kinds of difficulties later on. Wherever your model is sitting or standing you will find a shadow linking it up, across the carpet or floor and then on to some piece of furniture perhaps or a wall. Although it is not always obvious to the eye it is invariably there if you look for it. Again, often the whole of the shadow side of your figure links up at the feet or below the waist with a large shadow under the chair or table or on the wall. Look for this shadow because it is most useful in giving the figure substance, so that it belongs to those things around it. Look at the sepia drawings of Rembrandt for the greatest and most exquisite rendering of this problem. Although they are in sepia they are unbelievably lovely and in some strange way they are full of all the feeling of colour and life.

The early English water-colourists use this method of laying in —the monochrome first, leaving the colour work until after the whole picture has been built up both in drawing and tone.

Look at the figure work of Gainsborough, Hogarth, and of course Rowlandson—especially the latter as his application of colour and line is masterly and combines the interest of a Breughel with the finest water-colour technique.

Try painting a friend by gas or lamplight with heavy shadows thrown from the figure on to chair and background. Build from the study upwards with lovely fresh washes of colour—as light as you can possibly make them.

PORTRAIT PAINTING

For portraits you must of course have a model. But then you really don't have to look farther than yourself for that. A piece of mirror propped up in a good light and you have a model—temperament permitting—that is guaranteed to hold the pose. On the other hand, you may be fortunate enough to have a friend who does not mind being stared at from close range.

Place yourself fairly near him—not farther than, say, six or seven feet. Also you should try to get a strong light either above or on one side of the head. An accomplished painter would be able to tackle a portrait—even if the shadows are all ironed out by suffused lighting, but for the beginner it will be much easier if the model is placed so that there is definitely a shadow side to the head. The classical lighting is usually about 45° from above and to one side of the front of the head—look at the portraits by Reynolds and Velasquez to see this point made clear time and time again. Next you need to make yourself comfortable with your board at a reasonable angle to allow easy work and an uninterrupted view of your sitter.

You might make a few little notes to begin with to familiarize yourself with the eyes, nose and any other feature that interests you. When you come on to actually painting the head you will require a half-sheet Imperial paper and for practice and economy you should place your paper lengthwise so you can get at least two studies on the sheet. The size should be about half life-size which is something like five inches from top to chin. The best position is generally a three-quarter view—unless the model has a particularly fine profile. But this rule does not apply always and you should be free to choose whatever position for the head would please you. While practising you will want to find out as much as you can about the forms of the various features; for instance, how the eyes are drawn; the turn of the nostrils and the crease and form of the lips, together with the modelling of the ears.

Before I leave this preparation for the portrait I should stress that too much shadow on your model's head would be fatal. There should be much more in light than in shadow. Again do not have the model staring back at you—but have him fix his eyes on a point perhaps behind your own head or your own shoulder—something they can register their gaze upon, such as a window-frame or door-knob. Thus after he has had a rest, which should be the case every three-quarters of an hour if possible, and more if convenient, he will automatically know on what to look to regain the pose.

Now let us do a portrait. The first thing you would do after having drawn in the framework is gently to damp the paper. While this is drying out you can occupy yourself with mixing a general flesh colour that will float over the whole of the flesh area, except the hair and the whites of the eyes. This general colour is invariably warm and very light in tone. Though there are exceptions to this, you will need to be observant for if your model is very fair or a dark swarthy type you will obviously have to mix a general flesh colour to match. Usually a little yellow ochre or raw sienna with a touch of vermilion will do for this mixture. With the redder type you might find that light red or even crimson can be exchanged for vermilion.

Having done this, and while it is drying, you should mix a general colour from the shadows and shadow side of the head.

Sometimes the particular colour of the hair is approximate in tone to this colour and you can do the hair and shadow side in one operation. This rarely happens, but if it should, do not be afraid of mixing plenty of colour up and running the one into the other.

The general shadow colour is usually raw umber with a little light red to make it warmer or a tiny touch of Prussian blue to cool it. The latter will give it a slightly greenish quality which is exactly the colour required, especially with the darker types. Even with fair ones there is sometimes a suspicion of pale green, possibly in the neck or where the form goes away into the shadows. If you see green you must be honest to your vision and paint it in as green as you see it.

Next, go back into the hair if the colour is anything other than the colour of the shadows. With hair, especially the hair of children and young girls, I have found it best to tackle the problem in one go, i.e., to paint it in and finish it if possible in one session. The reason is plain to see once you come to paint a person with lots of hair, and perhaps curly hair, too, because you will want to make it all appear as one, not as something in a series of jagged steps, which so often happens when attempting to paint curls on to a dry colour. For instance, should your sitter's hair be brown, mix sufficient general colour in your pan and boldly float in the area of the hair except the parting, if this is very obvious. Then take the lights out with a dry brush.

For this operation I have found that a Hog brush is a most useful aid. Any old Hog brush will do, providing it is clean. With this you can manœuvre the colour off with sometimes greater success than with the less strenuous sables. Go for the big lights, and not single strands in light.

Then go back into the darks. You may have to mix something very much darker than the general colour mixed with blue or black. With rich brown hair sometimes a touch of crimson alizarine will be sufficient to give your brown the necessary punch.

When you come to those parts where the hair melts into the temple or the line of the forehead, you may need to do a little softening of the edge with a moist brush. But do be careful to use clean water when you moisten the brush; any muddiness coming into the flesh is a great trouble and often difficult to get out.

Also the head may have a halo of light around it, or at least a fuzzy or soft edge at the side or on the top, so there is bound to be a little softening somewhere on the hair.

With the general colour, lights and shadows completed, the hair should be looking almost finished. There may perhaps be a few small touches here and there which you can now go about, using a quite small brush to select a curl or a few strands of hair that catch the eye.

If the hair is fair, the problem is a little more difficult, if only because the difficulties cannot always be seen so soon. With black hair, for instance, you can see the general shape and the bluish highlight. But with the fairer type it is far more subtle.

When mixing your general colour be careful to get the colour right, and certainly not too dark, even if you fall into the error of making it too light. That is better than making it otherwise. Sometimes the general colour is about the same tone as the face and neck. If you make a good job of mixing the general colour of hair and flesh, you are well on the way to success.

Now you can begin to model the features in, still using a fairly large brush. Have plenty of colour on it, always being ready to mop up or take off (with your blotting paper handy) should you judge hastily, or wrongly.

Some painters would now go on to the eyes and finish them off, and then the nose, followed by the lips, but I would recommend the student to model the larger planes in first. Get some solidity into the head first before troubling with the details, modelling the brow to flow round on either side of the temples, also the cheeks, chin and neck. Put a touch of crimson or vermilion on the cheeks, should they be rosy, and carefully work it to fuse with the general flesh colour. Sometimes a little light red is better than crimson: it depends of course on the model's complexion whether they are fair or ruddy in colouring. When you have modelled the largest planes, rounding them carefully with a moist brush into the adjoining plan, you can then go on to paint the eyes, nose, lips, etc.

One word about the general colour lay-in The practice of the early English portraitists, using oils, of course, was to dab a touch of pink or rose colour on forehead, cheek, nose and chin: the reason for this is that in those parts of the face there is usually a certain amount of warmth Putting it in to begin with was merely their way of ensuring that it was not forgotten during the modelling of the forms when the painter is concerned with the drawing and modulations of the flesh to the detriment, possibly, of good colour.

Eyes are not so difficult as they look. The student must always remember to draw them in first and then build them up with colour. The common fault in the treatment of eyes is to distort the size of the iris leaving little or no room for the whites of the eye. To make it easier for the student to grasp this point I would ask him, when getting his model to pose for him, to take a three-quarter view, but with the model looking in his direction, but a little past him. In this way he should get plenty of white showing in the sitter's eyes.

When you come to paint in the iris itself, observe exactly where the highlight comes: it is usually less light than your white paper, but you should carefully leave the paper bare where the light comes, so that you can gently tone it down later, should you wish to do so.

If you look carefully at the eyes you will observe that the shadow under the top lid connects itself with the dark of the iris. This is an important point to look out for, as it helps to give the effect of the top lid projecting slightly over the eye. Do not worry too much about eyelashes unless they are extremely noticeable and large, and also do not attempt to paint them hair for hair. Try for the effect they make rather than for the correct number of hairs. The

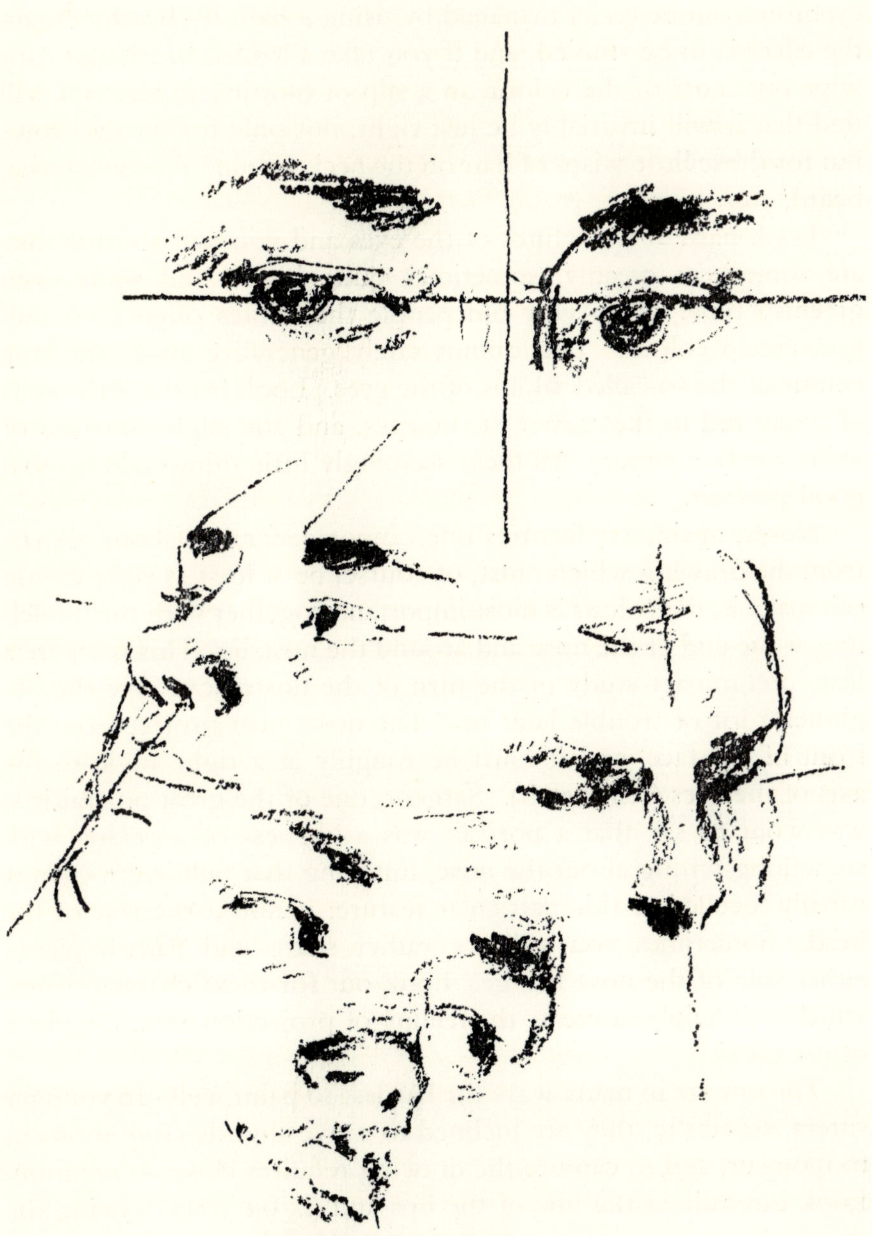

STUDIES FOR PORTRAIT

eyebrows can be easily managed by using a half-dry brush. Again the effect is to be studied, and if you take a loaded brush and then wipe out most of the colour on a slip of blotting paper, you will find that it will invariably be just right, not only for the eyebrows but for those little wisps of hair on the neck, around the moustache, beard, etc.

Look hard at the whites of the eyes and you will see that they are sometimes creamy, sometimes quite bluish and some even greenish blue. With very old people the whites often go a dull grey-cream colour. You cannot safely generalize about the true colour of the so-called whites of the eyes. Look for the little wells of pinky red in the corner of the eyes, and any slight blueness of vein near the corner. All these seemingly little things add up to a good portrait.

Noses, again, are features one cannot generalize about. Apart from the drawing which must, of course, be at least as right as you can make it, the colour is most important, together with the modelling at the end of the nose and around the nostrils. This is where a little preliminary study of the turn of the nostril can save the beginner a lot of trouble later on. The nose must project from the front of the face, and it must be roughly at a right angle to the axis of the eyes (see sketch). Sargent, one of the great portraitists, was wont to say that a portrait was a likeness of a person with something wrong about the nose, implying that public criticism is usually levelled at this particular feature, if not at the rest of the head. Sometimes you will see rather sharp and flattish planes either side of the nose bridge. Look out for these characteristics, which will help you create the feeling of projection from the plane of the cheek.

The lips are in many ways the hardest to paint well. In younger sitters, especially, they are inclined to move slightly from moment to moment, and to capture the drawing requires close observation. Look carefully at the line of the lips and fix on your drawing the position between nose and chin first; then at the overall width of the lips either side of a centre point immediately below the nose. This is the most important point, and the rest will follow with less trouble if you first fix accurately these points. The colour range of lips is tremendous from palest rose to vermilion; from pale mauve to carmine, and the texture differs from one to another just as widely. So be observant and if you see any points such as a highlight or reflected light upon them—providing that it is obvious—do your best to capture it in your study.

If your sitter is bearded (a delightful thing to tackle), the procedure is much as I have suggested for the painting of the hair. But when you come to join the beard to the lower cheeks and chin, you will perhaps have to use a lot of softening as well as the half-dry brush.

If your model has a moustache, then there will possibly be a shadow under the centre of the upper lip, and perhaps over the lower lip also. The same applies under the eyebrow: a shadow may pass across the top eyelid; and if your model is an old man with bushy eyebrows they may even put a slight shadow over the whole of the eye socket, which would mean that you would have to drop the tone of the "whites" and highlight accordingly.

Try to get a child of about ten or twelve to sit for you. Boys and girls of this age are ideal models, for they often take a great interest in what is going on and their colouring is a delight to paint.

Everything has a lustre—hair, eyes, lips and cheeks—and should you have a young girl, the chances are that you might have a bright piece of ribbon in her hair which adds greatly to the joy of painting. Be careful, but not afraid, and take plenty of colour on your brush. The water must be clean—which is no problem when working at home, where you can change it every half-hour or so. This is most important for portraiture, and perhaps more important because the freshness of flesh painting in water-colour can only be achieved if you mix your various colours and tints with clean waters.

ARCHITECTURAL LANDSCAPE

DURING the last century a popular and most enjoyable hobby for both young and old alike was to journey with a sketch-pad to the sights of Europe. Paestum, Pompeii, Rome and Florence were full of people bent on making a record, usually in water-colour or pencil, of the treasures of Antiquity. The advent of the mass-produced camera may have led to a lessening of interest in this pleasurable pastime. But since the last war a growing number of people have returned, sketch-book in hand, to paint those very things the camera does in a split second. The reason surely is that a snap does not tell us much about anything of artistic value, whereas an hour's drawing can explain worlds, should the artist be interested and able.

It is this form of painting that prompts me to add this chapter. It is for the amateur intending to paint on holiday places of historic or artistic interest, or the serious student desirous of painting landscapes featuring architectural motifs—cathedrals, castles, factories, bridges, etc.

Strictly speaking, should the buildings be some distance away, they would fall into the landscape-painting category. But obviously, should the cathedral, or whatever you are painting occupy the entire energy and interest, as well as the picture space, then it would cease to be landscape pure and simple.

The reason for painting a church, cathedral, bridge or some ancient Greek ruin may be that the artist wants a record of it for its value as an architectural piece, or because it gives him inspiration through the disposition of light, form and colour. Though one could make a highly detailed water-colour of the Acropolis, or St. Peter's, Rome, there would be every bit as much pleasure to the painter in tackling a bomb-site overgrown with grass and London Pride.

The London squares are comparatively unexplored by the painters of the metropolis, and one wonders how Vuillard, Manet and Monet would react to them in spring or winter.

But where one can to a certain extent be vague and woolly in drawing when painting distant hills, trees, woods, etc., and get away with it, no such luck surrounds the painting of buildings. The nearer they are the more it applies; the forms become more and more fore-shortened while the detail comes into sharper relief.

The student must therefore be careful not to position himself in such a way that the perspective appears tremendously foreshortened and difficult to manage. Don't make difficulties for yourself by taking on something which is obviously beyond your powers to draw. But should you be determined to paint a building, even though its perspective is complicated and difficult to grasp, then make notes about it first. Accustom yourself to the problems on a rough piece of paper or on your sketch-book where it doesn't matter how messy the drawing might come in the process of getting it right.

Once you are happy about the main points and masses, and certain in your mind where they vanish, then and then only should you jump into the business of colour.

Generally speaking, the treatment of architectural motives depends, apart from the composition, on verticals and horizontals. These may or may not be in perspective; if they are, then the vanishing in perspective of parallel lines is something the student must study.

This is where the constant making of notes in a sketch-book will bring its own reward. For perspective is something that you just cannot afford to play with—you either know where such and such a line is going, or vanishing or you do not. As far as the verticals are concerned, you are safe to draw them in vertical, unless of course you are painting from a high window or parapet from which you see buildings far beneath you. In this case the parallel sides of the building (which are, of course, in strict elevation, vertical) will converge the farther they go away from you and seem to widen as they come towards you, for the principles of perspective apply to verticals as much as they do to horizontals. But whereas you can check with your eye a horizontal line which ends on the horizon, this is far more difficult when looking up or down at verticals.

If you have set yourself down at the end of the village street, or to one side of the village square, you will notice that not all the buildings are of the same height. Yet allowing for the fact that all of them are horizontal or parallel with the ground, which includes the line of windows, roofs, etc., they would all be vanishing to a common vanishing point, if they were in line with each other. Those that are not, would go to another vanishing point on the horizon. So you will have to familiarize yourself with this point as early as possible whatever you are painting.

Interiors are one of the most enjoyable and rewarding subjects for the water-colourist to choose. The dark richness of the shadows, velvety and mysterious, relieved here and there by soft grey walls, is something that has always appealed to the painter's eye.

There are notable water-colour interiors by many artists that would well repay your attention. Look at the interiors of Russell Flint for their treatment and scale of brushwork. Disregard the figurework for a moment and view his paintings simply for the brilliant way the walls, roof and floor have been treated. Other notable examples to study are the water-colours of Muirhead, Bone and Sargent. Among contemporary painters look for the interiors of John Ward, whose delicate handling is well worth a closer study. Here you have a different approach in that the basic ingredient is draughtsmanship, clothed with pale colour applied wherever it is needed, freely and untickled.

If your interest lies out of doors towards the painting of cathedrals, castle walls, etc., then you should study the work of the early English masters such as Girtin and De Wint. Observe how the detail of window, door or turret has been handled, together with the scale of the original drawings. These are often very small indeed, yet they are precise and masterly in their simplicity of means.

For those students who are fortunate enough to get out into the country, the sight of outhouses is surely enough to set them painting. Nothing is so paintable, and the colour—usually dull brick—can be applied quickly and with gusto. Quarry work, brickworks and wharves are also ready-made subjects, as are port installations and marshalling yards.

Unless you have chosen as your subject a view of St. Paul's or Westminster Abbey in which the detail would require you draw it carefully to begin with, you can often tackle a piece of architecture with a minimum of scaffolding. First, get the general proportions in pencil and take a chance with the details within the big framework, relying on your eye alone for accuracy. It may not always perhaps be a success doing it that way, but only practice will make you perfect.

Enjoy yourself! There are few things in life so enjoyable as an afternoon spent water-colour sketching, on the banks of the river away from the crowd, where the water is green, or deep in the country stealing apples from nature's orchard, as it were, with your paint-box beside you and the sky above.